Tennis My Way

TENNIS MY WAY

Martina Navratilova

with *MARY CARILLO*

PHOTOGRAPHS BY KIMBERLY BUTLER

Charles Scribner's Sons   New York

Copyright © 1983 Martina Enterprises, Inc.

Library of Congress Cataloging in Publication Data

Navratilova, Martina, 1956–
Tennis my way.

Includes index.
1. Tennis. I. Carillo, Mary. II. Title.
GV995.N38 1983   796.342′2   83-11673
ISBN 0-684-18003-0

This book published simultaneously in the
United States of America and in Canada—
Copyright under the Berne Convention.

1 3 5 7 9 11 13 15 17 19   F/C   20 18 16 14 12 10 8 6 4 2

Printed in the United States of America.

The photo of Robert Haas and Martina Navratilova appears
courtesy of Robert Haas.

Here is to all the people who have over the years
helped me with forming my game and later
defining and perfecting it to its present state.

Contents

Introduction

I think that just by watching people you can tell what they are like inside. You sense what they think of themselves by their walk, their clothes, their signature, the way they enter a room or drive a car or compete in sports. Personalities are formed very early in life. My mom told me that when I was three years old I was quite shy but always running all over the place, fearlessly, and always smiling. When I began to play tennis at age five, I wanted to learn how to rush the net before I'd learned how to stay back on the baseline. I was constantly charging in. It was what my heart told me to do.

Tennis was not my first love. My family lived in the Krkonoše mountains in Czechoslovakia the first four years of my life, and we all learned to ski well. The maternal side of my family is the more athletic side, and my mother, Jana, encouraged me to ski, skate, and run all over the mountainside. My mother had excelled in gymnastics, cross-country skiing, downhill racing, and tennis, and my grandmother, Agnes Semanska, was ranked in Czechoslovakia's tennis top ten for a few years. My favorite sport of all was ice hockey. It seemed the most exciting sport and the Czechs were very good

1

at it, but it was hardly a sport for girls. So I skied a lot, and had I spent the rest of my life in the mountains, I guess I would have become a skier. When I was five years old, there were three indoor tennis courts in Prague. My stepfather used to haul clay there, and I would sneak onto the courts when no one was watching and play against the wall. I had no forehand and a two-handed backhand, but I loved to volley off the wall. One day, when I was seven, the woman who ran the indoor courts saw me hitting against the wall and encouraged me to use the courts. My stepfather then began to teach me how to play after he had finished working. I remember that the courts were so cold in the wintertime that sometimes I would play with a hat on and a glove on my right hand. My stepfather worked with me until I was nine, and by then, I had driven him crazy with my stubborn attack on the net. He would try to lay down some fundamentals—solid groundstrokes, a nice steady game—but I was always eager to finish a point with a volley. He tried to discourage me by explaining that I was far too small to adopt that kind of style. And I *was* small. Until I was about fourteen I was usually the second or third shortest kid in the class. But I was not about to change my opinion on how the game should be played, and, fortunately, a fine coach named George Palma gave me instruction and improved my technique.

My stepfather began to take me to tournaments when I was nine, but some tournament officials denied my entry, saying that I was too small and that I would have to wait until I got bigger. Even my stepfather worried about me, and on very hot days he would actually hose my head off on changeovers so I wouldn't overheat. We traveled to tournaments all over Czechoslovakia on a 175cc motorcycle, the kind that goes only about fifty miles an hour. We would tie my two tennis rackets to the back of the bike and travel as far as two hundred miles from home. For the next five years I took a lot of losses, but I also knew I was getting better, especially since at one event we ran out of money. My mom had to come and rescue us, bringing more money for expenses and some Wiener schnitzels. We just hadn't figured that I would advance so far in that tournament.

At fourteen I was the national champion for that age group, and at sixteen the Czech Tennis Federation allowed me to play tennis in the United States. It was at the time of the then-new Virginia Slims Circuit, the women's first professional tour, starring Billie Jean King, Rosie Casals, and Margaret Court. I had an uncle in Canada who subscribed to *World Tennis* magazine, and he would send me his issues and I would devour the pages, learning everyone's name and all of the results. My idols became Billie Jean, Margaret Court, and Rod Laver. More than anything I wanted to play like Laver did, but my style was more similar to Margaret's, the idea being to serve hard and barrel into the court on everything.

I wanted to play against these players. I wanted to wear Virginia Slims dresses and play to the crowds and be a professional tennis player. But the federation did not recognize professional tennis and instead entered me in the USTA (United States Tennis Association) circuit, where I remained an amateur. In 1973 my daily expense money was eleven dollars, except in New York, where it was upped to thirteen dollars a day. (Even in Czechoslovakia people knew that life was more expensive in the Big Apple.) I saved a lot of my expense money by eating constantly at the courts, where meals were often given to the players. I remember walking to a grocery store in Fort Lauderdale, Florida, with another Czech player, Maria Neumannova, and buying some cheese, milk, ham, and orange juice, and the bill came to five dollars. Five dollars represented two days' work to my stepfather, and I had trouble seeing around that fact. But by the end of the trip I was spending twenty dollars a day for food and not even thinking about it. The food was so plentiful and tasted so good that I gained twenty pounds inside of three weeks. Everyone was commenting on it, but I was pleased with the change. I thought I looked a lot more feminine that way because I was no longer bony and sharp and strictly made of muscles.

During the next two years I became one of the best woman tennis players in the world and I was loving everything about it. I was speaking good English, I had adopted American slang, music, food, and clothes as my own, and my friends were Americans—Billie Jean, Rosie, and Chris Evert. And then the Czech Federation began to restrict my travel. They claimed that I had gotten lazy, that I had become too Americanized, and that I should be hanging around only with other European players. They were even going to deny me a chance to play in the 1975 U.S. Open, but, fortunately, Jan Kodes, a top-ranking Czech player at the time, intervened on my behalf.

It was at the U.S. Open that I defected. When I think about it now I recognize the magnitude of the decision and see how big a deal it really was, but at the time I did not. I knew that I was leaving my parents, but even that fact did not sink in until it became a reality. I never dreamed the whole thing would attract so much attention, that letters written home would be opened and edited, that the press would be somewhat hostile, that my own country would denounce me and ignore my achievements. But I wanted to live in America, to travel as I pleased, and, more than anything, I wanted to be number one in the world. I had made my choice.

It was then that I met Sandra Haynie, the pro golfer, and we became good friends. Sandra was a very good influence on me. She was what I was not—cool, calm, and controlled—and her peaceful life-style rubbed off on me. She became my manager and looked out for me, but I was still highly undisciplined. When I wasn't playing tennis I didn't practice much at all. I spent my free time shopping and relaxing, and, despite this passive regimen, I was ranked number one in the world in 1978 and 1979. I thought it would never end. It didn't quite work out that way, because when you are number one, the whole world wants to beat you. I know that now, but I had grown complacent at the top and stopped producing number-one tennis. By 1980 I was ranked third in the world and I was miserable.

In the spring of 1981 I met Nancy Lieberman, the basketball star. She watched me lose a pretty big match at Amelia Island and was surprised. Later at the French Open she saw me practice for about thirty minutes on a day off and could not believe that I then proclaimed myself ready to play the match the next day. After a disastrous stretch of losing four tournaments without ever reaching the finals, the last being Wimbledon, she came over to me and said, "What is this? Aren't you supposed to be real good or something?" Here was someone who had spent many hours every day trying to perfect herself in her craft, and when she witnessed my blithe approach to my sport she thought I was kidding. She began to help me, and her friendship has changed my life around.

A few weeks after meeting Nancy I left for the European circuit. I came home from Wimbledon a losing semifinalist, the same as the year before. Nancy did not know much about tennis, but she knew that Wimbledon is the most important event of the year. She made me get down to work. My attitude started to change and I realized that I needed help with my game if I wanted to take my best shot at regaining the number-one ranking and staying there. At the 1981 U.S. Open Renee Richards, a fine player and brilliant tactician, began coaching me, and from there I was on my way.

With Renee and Nancy I relearned and rethought everything I ever knew about the game. I learned that matches are won on the practice court, in the gym, and in the mind. I was taught that I have to make my practice sessions twice as tough as my matches so that the matches are easy, physically and mentally. This idea was totally new to me, and even now, no matter how hard I try, how much I concentrate, I cannot put out as much in practice as I do in a match. The excitement is not there, nor is the pressure, and there are no fans when I train. The electric atmosphere of a packed arena is only a memory, and out of the glare of the spotlight I cannot help relaxing mentally. That little bit of extra I can summon from somewhere deep inside myself is missing when the sincere need for it is absent, but I have learned to get as close as possible to the feel of a match so that when I play for real I do not suddenly have to create a physical and mental edge—I only have to recall it. I have learned how to pay my dues, and this is the challenge to be faced by every athlete. You, too, must get to the point in practice where you are not resenting, dreading, or getting bored by the work. You must challenge your own psyche.

I am still very much a person of the heart, and this will never change. But trying to play on instinct and talent alone was not enough to stay number one. I now know what it takes to be a true champion, and if I can help someone to find the champion in herself, this book will be worth the effort.

Equipment

When I was small and just starting to play in Prague, I had only one pair of shorts and two shirts. Only one of the shirts looked good enough to play a match in, so every night I would wash out my match outfit. These days, boxes of clothes arrive at my house in every color and every combination, but I still remember my shorts from the old days. Growing up I never had two rackets of the same make either, so if a string broke on my favorite, I'd have to adjust to my spare racket—a tricky business. Not until I was thirteen did I get a popular racket, Dunlop, supplied to me by the Tennis Federation.

I always played with wooden rackets when I was growing up, for the simple reason that at the time wood was the only material rackets were made from. After a while some manufacturers started making metal rackets—the Wilson T2000, which Billie Jean King used for a while (and Jimmy Connors still uses), the Slazenger Steels, and the Lacoste steel frame. Because I had grown up with the feel of wood, I never considered switching. But the trend continued, and from 1974 to 1976 I played with a Fiberglas, open-throated racket. In those three years I was continually bothered by shoulder problems, inflammation caused by the vibration of the composite frame, and I switched back to wood. I figured it was for good, that no composite racket could afford me the same feel and response as the natural properties of wood, but after two more years of wood playing I experimented a little bit more. The Yonex racket company had increased their line of frames considerably, and like many other manufacturers had developed a midsize composite. They asked me to try it out, and although I thought I couldn't play without wood, within five minutes of using their racket, I knew I had found a great one. It was only ten days before the 1982 French Open, the biggest clay court championship in the world, and many would think it a curious time to experiment with such an important piece of equipment. But I truly believed in the benefits of the racket, and not only did I use the Yonex to win Paris, but Wimbledon as well. I have a feeling I'll be hanging onto this one for a while. Actually, Renee Richards told me all along I would love the racket.

Rackets

Choosing the proper frame is a highly individualistic business, one that requires a bit of experimentation. With so much to choose from these days in terms of racket size, weight, material, and balance, it becomes a question of what you alone find yourself most comfortable with. There seems to be too much emphasis placed on the brand names of rackets, and certainly on the prices. Do not buy a racket solely for status. A three- or four-hundred-dollar racket may not do a thing for your game, but a forty-dollar racket may bring out your best tennis. If the racket you use gives you a sense of confidence, chances are it is just fine.

There are three sizes of rackets made today—the traditional size, the midsize, and the oversize. Fewer and fewer pros seem to use the traditional-size frames these days when the larger rackets promise a greater hitting area, more power, and more confidence in each swing. The racket I use is a midsize, and I am not at all aware of the added size of it, a complaint some players have about the bigger frames. Some oversized rackets are in fact too cumbersome, and those of you who have trouble with maneuverability at the net may find this a problem. The bigger rackets are a great help at the net, but you need quick hands to reap the benefits. I've also noticed that some topspin players have difficulty using oversized rackets; they seem to have difficulty with the added bulk and cannot whip around the ball well enough to impart topspin. Again, experiment. There are usually test rackets at any pro shop. Or borrow a friend's frame for a few days and give it a good, all-around hit. If you were always a bit reluctant to venture up to the net behind your serve, you may discover extra guts when you've got a big racket head leading the charge forward.

Handle Sizes

Once again, comfort is the name of the game. I've got a much bigger hand than Chris Evert Lloyd, but I use a smaller size grip than she does. I feel that I've got better touch with more hand on the racket with a small handle. Some pros feel that a bigger handle keeps the hand from turning as much on impact. Whatever size you decide on, make sure you do not lose your grip because of an improper-size handle. Be aware that handles come in several different shapes—round, square, octagonal, or built up. If you tend to have difficulty switching from one grip to another, it may help a lot to use a handle with multiple planes, such as the flat, square grip or the octagonal.

Weight of the Racket

Rackets can weigh from twelve to about fourteen ounces. A few ounces may not seem like much of a difference, but don't be fooled. A heavier racket does not mean that you will hit a heavier ball, or that a light racket is just for kids. The momentum you achieve from swinging the racket is what gives your stroke its follow-through. Heavy rackets could easily inhibit your swing, just as light rackets could whip through the air and sabotage your follow-through for the opposite reason.

Make sure your racket is not causing you to become arm-weary or forcing you to muscle the ball around. If you're a wristy player you will probably have an easier time with a lighter racket. If you are strong and enjoy hitting the ball flat, you may appreciate a heavier model. What is very important to remember is that the hand-me-down routine in rackets is a big mistake. Never give a young child one of your old frames to play with if it's at all heavy. Not only could it hurt the child physically by straining and exhausting arm muscles, but also it could greatly hamper her play and discourage the child from the game entirely. There are junior-size rackets that are lighter and shorter than standard size, with smaller handles, too. I think it makes a lot of sense to scale down the equipment according to size. Most other sports, such as baseball and hockey, adapt equipment to suit the needs of the players, and tennis should as well.

The Balance of a Racket

While balance is not spoken about much, the pros are sensitive to the balance of their frames. Most amateur players are not aware of racket balance at all, because the distribution of weight in a racket is not the kind of information normally included on the side of the frame. Basically a racket can be balanced evenly, head-heavy, or handle-heavy. Most rackets are evenly balanced. Some players, in an effort to beef up their swings and follow-throughs, look specifically for a racket that has more weight toward the head so that the racket will swing through the air at an accelerated rate. Most of the pros like the weight down toward the handle or dead even. Women especially lean toward a racket that allows for good handling at the net, and a frame that is too head-heavy could draw errors. Make certain this is not the case with your racket.

Stiff or Flexible?

Individual preference again comes into play with the flexibility of a racket, but you should know what kind of frame would complement your style of play. If you play with a lot of control but do not generate much power, a flexible frame could help. Steel rackets are by far the most flexible, with the composites coming in second, and most wood frames last. If you've got the power but lack the control, wood rackets could help, or the stiff composites, but stay away from the steel frames or you'll be launching balls into orbit.

Types of Strings

There are two types of strings—gut and nylon. Tournament players use gut strings. Genuine gut has a natural feel and resiliency that the pros rely on, and we tend to get very picky about our gut. Once the gut gets a little wet (a few minutes of rain will do), the feel of the strings is damaged for good. This can be an expensive proposition, which is why nylons and synthetic-gut strings are so popular these days. These strings are far less expensive, and the new nylon strings are just as playable as gut, so I would recommend them over anything else. But if gut is what you want, know the different gauges it comes in. A fifteen-gauge gut is thicker than the sixteen- and seventeen-gauge guts. For the average player, the fifteen-gauge gut makes the most sense because it lasts longer. Remember, gut will cost much more than nylon. I personally like a sixteen light-gauge gut. I feel the ball better on these strings, and I think the thinness takes the spin of the ball better, too.

Tension of the Strings

First things first. Do not buy a racket that is sitting in a store, already strung. Who knows how long it has been there? The strings could be brittle and the racket may have warped. Purchase the racket first, then decide how you would like it strung. Fortunately, when you buy a racket these days you are usually given a recommended tension for the strings, but feel free to experiment with the playability of the racket at different tensions. When I play on the faster surfaces, such as carpet and grass, I string my racket tight. On clay courts I use a looser-strung frame, because with looser strings the ball will stay on the racket a fraction of a second longer. I like this on clay courts, where I tend to have to hit the ball harder to make it go farther. If I am playing with heavy balls, I like my strings a little looser as well, and with a light ball my strings will be tight. But now we are really talking about minor points of the game. Do not vary the tension of your strings so much that you are forced to change your strokes in any important way. A few pounds of tension are all we're really discussing. For the most part my racket is strung at about seventy-two pounds of pressure.

Tennis Balls

As if this game weren't complicated enough, now even the balls you buy come in various categories. There are high-pressure balls for altitude tennis, allowing for a five-thousand-foot jump in elevation. There are heavy-duty balls made with extra felt that are designed for hard-court tennis, where the ball really takes a beating. There are balls specifically made for grass courts, clay courts, and indoor courts. There are different-colored balls for added visibility and recognizability, and there's even a multicolored ball that, the manufacturers claim, improves concentration by allowing the player to see the spin on the ball. I don't know about that, but I do know that when the balls get too soft, throw them out. The bounce of dead balls can throw off your game and seriously hurt your arm. A dead and heavy ball will make you labor with your strokes and can toss off your rhythm and fluidity in no time. So when in doubt, toss the ball out.

Clothing

All tennis clothing should be very comfortable and cool. Tennis used to be a game with all-white clothing, but these days colored clothing is just as popular. When in sunlight, just remember that white reflects it, while colors absorb it. If you tend to perspire a lot, use sweatbands and headbands. Headbands are also useful in keeping your hair out of your face, and when I play in the wind I wear one. A tennis hat will keep you cool and absorb sweat as well.

When it's cold, wear warm-ups before and after you play. As you begin to warm up, gradually remove clothing—the warm-up jacket, a sweater, and finally your warm-up pants. This will help prevent pulled muscles, bad backs, and colds. Forget about buying the expensive warm-up outfits. To my way of thinking, the warm tracksuits—the type with the hoods—are just great, and they cost less than fifteen dollars. I wear them more than anything else when I practice in the cold.

I have recently learned the benefits of wearing two or three pairs of socks when I play. This not only absorbs the terrible shock that your feet must endure out on the court, but it also helps to prevent blistering. I've also taken to wearing high socks in my practice sessions. These are not common in tennis, but they support calf muscles well and reduce the chances of injuries and cramping. With all of this sock action going on, you may have to buy tennis shoes a half size larger. One other tip: In hot weather put baby powder inside your shoes. It not only cools off your feet, but it actually reduces the friction inside your shoes, helping to prevent blistering.

Tennis Shoes

I wear out a pair of tennis shoes in three or four days, but I doubt that you will. Proper shoes are very important in all sports, and rarely are they interchangeable. Do not wear boat shoes or basketball shoes to play tennis. A good tennis shoe is specifically designed for tennis. The shoes should have cushioned arches and heels and be well balanced for quick turns. They should be comfortable and lightweight and able to last a long time. If you buy leather shoes, keep in mind that they will stretch a bit. I prefer mesh shoes. They are generally lighter and breathe better than leather shoes, and they tend to hold their shape longer as well.

Training and Conditioning

With my natural ability and strength I was able to get away with an awful lot for a long while. In 1975 and 1976 I was even getting away with being twenty-five pounds overweight. There was never enough stress put on physical conditioning when I was younger. A fitness program did exist for the top tennis players in Prague, but the instructors were largely untrained and more often than not they would just about kill us off with their crazy drills. We would use dead weights, jump over benches, and jog around aimlessly and forever, and I just hated it. All of this was once or twice a week —very informal stuff—and it didn't do a whole lot to help anyone's tennis game. Knowing what I know now, I only wish that I had spent my youth training properly. It has taken me a long time to develop my explosive style of play, a style that is mentally and physically exhausting and puts a premium on physical fitness. A few years back I was playing a match in Canada against Tracy Austin and at 6–5 in the first set I realized that I was already fatigued. It was then that I resolved never to lose a match to weariness. Fatigue produces errors. I did not consider the truth of this until I was twenty-five years old. The training

I do now has helped me immensely, and no matter what level player you are the proper tennis training will improve your game. It will greatly reduce your chances of injuries, too.

How I Train

Tennis is different from all other sports because there is no official off-season. Each individual player decides when he or she wants to play or rest, and there is a tournament somewhere every week of the year. I enjoy playing all year round, in all different countries, and on all different surfaces. This puts pressure on me to be fit all the time, and I try very hard to be just that. Hardly a day goes by that I am not somehow working on my fitness and strength.

If I did have an off-season, I would use the time to bulk up some with heavy weights and establish a rigorous running routine, but the nature of my business precludes this sort of training because the recovery time would be far too long. Instead, I train in intervals, some weeks very difficult and some just to maintain tone, some days with weight training and some with roadwork and other exercises. What I must keep in mind is that in a match lasting over three hours, the actual physical work—the running and hitting—amounts to something less than thirty minutes, so I must develop explosive power that I can sustain for an entire match. To this end, I train both on and off the court.

Off-Court Training

About three times a week I jog for two miles, sometimes more. I jog first thing, before I play any tennis, and it helps to loosen me up. About three days a week I will jump rope for about ten minutes, which I find is good not only for my timing but also for my quickness and hand movements. I do sit-ups every day, about a hundred of the tough ones—those that are done on your back with bent knees and the feet free, not hooked or held down by anything. This places all of the pressure on your stomach muscles, which is what you want. I rotate my clasped arms from side to side as I draw up from the sit-up so that different side muscles are being taxed on every set. I will do two sets of fifty or five alternating sets of twenty sit-ups. I am sure to do some reverse sit-ups as well so that my back muscles also will be exercised. Three sets of ten will do just fine.

Another way to exercise your stomach muscles without putting too much pressure on your lower back is to lie down, again with your knees bent, and then lift your back about five to seven inches off the ground and hold for about fifteen seconds. Do that about fifteen times, and then work your way up. Don't overdo it on the situps since it can shorten your stomach muscles and cause you to hunch over.

Every other day I do sprints. Before I begin, I slowly jog about 880 yards (half a mile) to warm up my body. Then I stretch a bit and follow that by some quick, high-stepping pumps in place. Then I start my sprints —440s, then some 220s, then 110s. On Monday I may do one of each; on Wednesday, six 110s; and so on. Some days I will work on speed, on others, endurance, but I try to lose all loose and extraneous movement in my running technique. I am searching for economy of motion. After the sprints I will again jog an 880 to warm down.

Every other day I will do some weight training. The weights are an integral part of my fitness program, and I am sure to utilize the weights correctly or else I could tear down and not build up my muscles. It has taken me about a year to get into proper shape through weight training, and now I basically am on a maintenance program that keeps my muscles toned. I will not deviate from this unless I am injured or ill for a time, in which cases I would isolate different muscle groups or restructure my program until I could achieve my present level once more. I always stretch before I use any weight equipment. I use Nautilus machines, a Cybex machine (which is electronically controlled resistance), some free weights, a Total Gym (which is a system of resistance pulleys), and a Hydrogym, which is a piece of hydraulic equipment offering six different resistance levels. I will do no heavy weight lifting at all the two days before or during a competition. My weight program has been specifically designed for my body's needs, and I want to stress that if you wish to get serious about training with weights you must talk to someone who knows what he or she is doing so that the person can design the proper weight program for your body.

The results of intelligent weight training may surprise you. On a per-ounce basis, girls' muscles are 10 percent stronger than those of boys, and although women cannot develop the same kind of musculature as men, in the same amount of time they can actually achieve greater strength increase.

If you have not done much weight training, the first thing to work on is the legs. The carry-over effort of conditioning is much more profound in the legs than in the arms. In developing your arms you accelerate your heart rate, which is a good cardiovascular workout as well as an arm-strengthening one, but once you are done with the training, the conditioning diminishes rapidly. The lower extremities sustain the benefits of the workouts a lot longer, so even modified versions of training programs will help your game.

My personal off-court training workout in the gym was created by David Balsley, a physical therapist who knows my body's strengths and weaknesses. (He says I can still use some work on my upper body.) It takes about thirty minutes to complete and I go through this nearly every day after I have finished practicing, but again during tournaments.

How to Stretch

Before we go on to the conditioning program, a word about stretching. Not only does stretching cut down on injuries, but also I have found that I play much better tennis when I am thoroughly limber. I am not flexible at all by nature, so I really take time to loosen up.

What doctors have recently found is that more injuries occur *after* and not during the time you play tennis. When you get off the court, if you take a shower and sit down, everything tightens up. For this reason I do my stretching after I practice training in the gym and after I get off the court.

I make certain to stretch out my back and groin muscles, hips, hamstrings, calves, and arm muscles. You should begin by holding a stretch for five to seven seconds, slowly and without any jerky motion or bouncing.

Fig. 1 *Shoulder and hamstring stretch*   Fig. 2 *Shoulder stretch*

Fig. 3 *Groin stretch*

Fig. 4
Thigh and groin stretch

Fig. 5 *Thigh stretch*

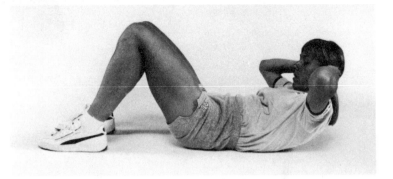

Fig. 6 *Sit-ups. Hold for five seconds ten times, then build up to ten seconds ten times, two to three times a day.*

Fig. 7 *Bicycle riding*

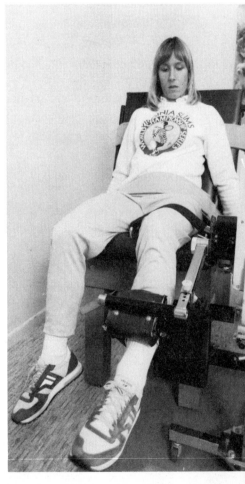

Fig. 8 *Weight training on the Cybex machine*

As you hold the stretches for a greater amount of time, you will increase your suppleness.

My Thirty-Minute Conditioning Program

This training program works on high, explosive energy. One exercise is followed by the next immediately, and, when done correctly, should take from twenty to thirty minutes.

1. *Bicycle riding.* This is to work up a sweat and get my leg muscles warm. I stay on the bike for about ten minutes at one speed, then do sprints; in a two-minute time frame I will sprint for three seconds, rest for seven. After that I am mildly warm. (Actually, I'm breathing hard.)
2. *Weights.* I use either Nautilus or Hydrogym equipment or a Cybex machine to work on my lower-extremity strength. I use fairly heavy weights, providing that I have no weaknesses in my legs at the time. If I've got a pull or strain somewhere, I will train specifically for that, using the Cybex machine to isolate the area of weakness. The amount of weight varies on each machine, as do the repetitions. Since a separate book could be written on this alone in order to do it properly, please consult a weight-training specialist who can set up the proper program for your build and needs.
3. *Arm drill.* This drill is a killer, and it sounds so easy. I stand in place for one minute while making very rapid arm motions as if running, pumping them up and down as fast as I can.

4. *Abdominal work.* Studies show that most of the speed and velocity built up by baseball pitchers and football quarterbacks comes not from the arm but from the rotation of the trunk. I do sit-ups—five or six different ways—to build up my abdominal muscles and trunk. By rotating differently every time you pull up from a sit-up, you work different trunk muscles. I will do modest sets of each different sit-up, some with arms crisscrossing, some straight up, some from an elevated plane. I do sit-ups every day, but what is important is that you do not do too many sit-ups at the same time and use the same muscles, or you will lose your stretching abilities. To prevent this, I sometimes throw in some reverse sit-ups—hyperextensives—so that my back muscles get some exercise as well.

5. *The stairs.* I run sprints up fifteen stairs. In about four minutes I will run these stairs about fifteen times. I skip every other step and jog on the way down. This works on leg speed, leg strength, and foot speed.

6. *Upper extremities.* This work is done on a piece of gym equipment called the Total Gym, a system of pulleys attached to a free-sliding plane that you sit on. In other words, when you pull on the hand lever you are sliding your own weight up and back. This makes for very good practice on forehands, backhands, and overheads (by lying on my back). I do three sets of ten on each stroke, sliding my weight up and back as I mimic my swing. This can be improvised at home if you can set up a system whereby your arm is constantly resisting a steady weight. I then do wrist curls. Using a bar of tubular metal, I turn the metal as fast as I possibly can, toward my body, then away from my body. The faster you try to rotate the bar, the harder you naturally grip it,

Fig. 9 *Running on the treadmill can be boring, but watching ESPN at the same time is not so boring*

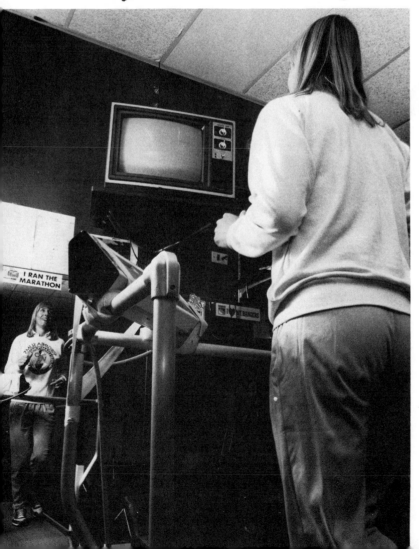

and by holding the bar straight out in front of your body you really feel a burn. I curl for about two minutes. You can also do this by squeezing a rubber ball.

7. *Jumping.* I jump in place on alternating legs, dropping deeply on each jump. I do three sets of twenty. I also do lateral jumping, which is jumping on one leg for three sets of twenty each. This is excellent for leg strength and balance.

8. *Running.* I run on a treadmill, uphill, for a mile or a mile and a half. I follow this with stretching, then move onto the court, where I work on speed and endurance.

On-Court Running Drills for Quickness and Endurance

I do on-court running drills after each practice session and during the first two or three days of an event, after which I will pull up a bit and save my energy for the final days' matches. These drills should be done one right after the other; the rest time is minimal and dependent upon the length of the drill. For instance, the first drill is very quick—about fifteen seconds—so that's how much recovery time you should allow yourself before going out. *All drills are done with racket in hand.*

1. This first drill is for developing explosive starts and stops to the ball. Sprint from the baseline to the service line and back five times, using quick pivots on each line. You should not need more than three or four steps to cover the distance each time.

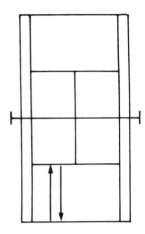

Drill 1

15 seconds

Back and forth 5 times.
All forward running with
quick pivots.

2. This drill is for both forward movement and back-pedaling and should take about thirty or thirty-five seconds to complete. Run forward from the baseline to the service line, backpedal back three times at top speed. Then run the distance from the baseline to the net the same way, also three times.

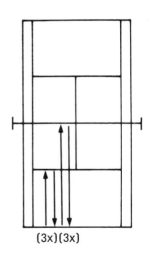

(3x)(3x)

Drill 2

30–35 seconds

Back and forth from
baseline to service line
3 times with
backpedaling.
Back and forth from
baseline to net 3 times
with backpedaling.

3. This is a lateral drill and mimics the movements you would make when running from side to side after a ball. Run the length of the baseline ten times, keeping in mind that, as in a match, you would be looking toward the court. Keep your balance sound, make dead starts and stops, and execute a shadow swing at the completion of every dash. Time on this is about thirty-five seconds.

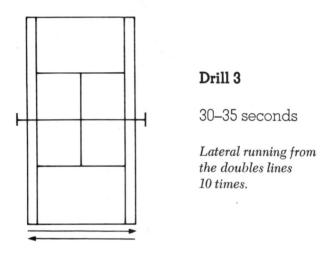

Drill 3

30–35 seconds

Lateral running from the doubles lines 10 times.

4. The fan drill helps forward running but especially stresses backpedaling, the kind of running you would use for overheads. This drill takes about forty seconds when done well, but it's pretty tough. Start from the middle of the court. Run forward to the left net post and backpedal to the center again. Then run to the center tape and back, then to the right net post and back. Then run back and forth from the far left service line, the middle service line, and the far right line. Upon completing these movements slide laterally from the center of the court to one end of the baseline, then the other, until you finish in the middle of the baseline.

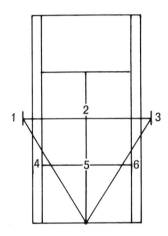

Drill 4   Fan Drill

40 seconds

Run forward and backward from each station.

5. The suicide drill is not named whimsically. It's a killer, but it brings out your forward speed, endurance, balance, and pivot power. My best time on this is about twenty-six seconds, and when I really want to go for the suicide and run through this twice, my time is pretty close to fifty seconds. This drill stresses strictly forward movements and sharp, clean pivots. First, sprint from the baseline to the service line and back. Second, sprint to the net and back. Third, sprint from the baseline to the opposite service line and back. Fourth, sprint from the baseline to the opposite baseline and back. If you go for it twice, reverse the order of sprints, from the longest to the shortest. Then collapse.

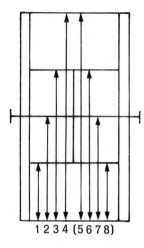

1 2 3 4 (5 6 7 8)

Drill 5   Suicide Drill

30 seconds once

60 seconds twice

*All running is forward,
with quick pivots.*

Obviously, the better shape you are in when you perform these drills, the more you can get out of them. It's a good idea to use a stopwatch so that you can gauge your improvements and try to beat your best times. Start slowly or you will feel the burn the next day. It is a good idea to do these drills when you switch from one surface to the next because footing is always different. I never skip these, and I find that the transitions from hard courts to clay to grass are far smoother because of the drills.

Reflex Training

The drills I do with Rick Elstein, a coach from New York, are designed specifically for sharper reflexes. The idea is to get me to see the ball early, react to it quickly, and execute efficiently.

In one drill, Rick will merely hit serves to me, varying the speed and the spin constantly and forcing me to react without any hesitation. I focus on the ball right from the toss and process the facts right off the strings of his racket, not with a wild guess. I pivot immediately, without confusion, and stroke smoothly.

The second drill is called the Goalie Drill, and for good reason. I stand a few feet in front of the net, facing my own baseline. Two markers are on either side of me, indicating the goal area that I must stand in front of and defend. Rick stands on the baseline with a bucket of balls and fires shots at my goal, balls that I must deflect away, hockey style, with my racket. Once you become good at this, the balls can come at you faster and faster and the goal markers can be spread farther and farther apart. This is a great drill, not only for sharpening reflexes but for covering the net area as well.

Nutrition

I was tagged early in my career as a real junk-food fanatic, constantly eating fast foods, pancakes, and everything else. In the past few years I had been trimming down considerably and attempting to eat more sensibly, but it was only after my bout with toxoplasmosis that I began to realize the importance of nutrition to my performance. Toxoplasmosis occurs when an offending organism, transmitted by raw meat, an infected cat, or any number of other ways, enters the bloodstream and produces a high level of antibodies. This causes muscle inflammation, muscle pain, and muscle weakness. I contracted toxoplasmosis in the summer of 1982 and lost to Pam Shriver in the U.S. Open quarterfinals. After the loss, Nancy Lieberman and I decided that one of the ways to build back strength was through proper nutrition. Through a mutual friend I met Robert Haas, a nutritionist who specializes in training athletes to eat correctly to achieve full potential and peak performance. I was very interested in what he had to say. I knew that he could not give me a better backhand or an angled serve, but I wanted to get a competitive edge through proper nutrition, and I did. I have increased my stamina, endurance, energy level, speed, strength, and neuromuscular coordination. I fully believe that sports nutrition will become an important aspect of athletic training, and I recommend such nutrition to anyone and everyone.

Robert designed the program I follow specifically for me, based on biological values he gleaned through various testing processes. He calls this "Nutritional Engineering," and although the basic principles are ironclad, the program changes according to blood chemistry, sex, age, the athlete's sport, and other variables. Into this dietary equation he adds my favorite foods so that I may indulge in them as well.

Peak-Performance Program

At the highest levels of the game the outcome is often decided by willpower and endurance. This means that the smallest improvement at the top, which for me is about 5 percent, can make all the difference in the world. The up-and-coming junior or the club player has much more room for improvement than this and should take advantage of that kind of potential.

Basically, my eating involves a high complex carbo-hydrate intake, with low fats and a moderate amount of protein. The complex carbohydrates are the starches —potatoes, pasta, breads, vegetables, fruits, grains, and cereals. The simple carbohydrates taste sweet, such as sugar, molasses, honey, and syrup, and have only a limited role in my diet. Though still allowed, they com-prise no more than 10 percent of my daily calories.

The fat content of athletes is critical. For optimal health and peak performance, total fat should be no more than 10 to 15 percent of your daily diet and no more than 20 percent for marathon runners. There are

Fig. 10 *Martina Navratilova and Robert Haas, her nutritionist*

two kinds of fats—saturated, which come from animals, and unsaturated, which come from vegetables. An excess of both is dangerous. Too much saturated fat can lead to heart disease and strokes, and too much unsaturated fat promotes cancer.

As far as protein is concerned, Americans tend to go way overboard. It is true that you need protein for body maintenance, repairs, and in order to keep the immune system running smoothly, but the average American eats far more protein than he needs per day. Too much protein retards and cripples an athlete's performance, though I should point out that in situations of stress and physical exertion the body needs more protein than normal.

Too much protein tends to dehydrate a body, which is the primary cause of decline in an athletic performance. This happens because a person urinates more frequently in order to excrete toxic protein by-products, losing not only water but also important vitamins and minerals from the system. Protein foods require seven times the amount of water needed to digest carbohydrates. In an effort to handle all the excess protein, the body draws water from working muscles and cells that need water most during an athletic performance. This in turn causes the body temperature to rise, which is also very debilitating.

In general, I say that you should cut down on protein and increase your complex carbohydrates. If you eat, say, 2,000 calories a day, 10 percent of that should be protein. If you go by gram measurement (you can purchase a simple food-composition book at a health-food store) you should not exceed between fifty and eighty grams of protein a day. Most Americans eat about one hundred. My own intake is about fifty, and depending on whether I am training or playing in a tournament, my intake will rise or fall.

As far as alcohol is concerned, this diet encourages near-teetotalism. In the body, alcohol is handled like sugar. It contains no nutrients at all and dehydrates the system, too. All alcohol gives you is calories. It also turns off a hormone made in the base of the brain called ADH. When a person drinks, it causes her body to excrete more water, causing dehydration and a loss of maximum aerobic capacity. Of course, you can get away with some alcohol intake, depending upon your blood chemistry and body weight. It's true that a heavier person can drink more than a lighter person, but whoever you are, alcohol will have a direct toxic effect on your liver, kidneys, and brain cells. It also raises the level of fat carried in the blood, can poison the blood if the level of alcohol is high enough, and raises the body's amount of uric acid, which could pre-dispose someone to gout. Fortunately for me, cutting out alcohol is no big deal. My alcohol consumption is exceptionally low, and the only things I will sometimes have are light beers and champagne—wine gives me a headache. In general you should never have more than one mixed drink and no more than a few light beers a night. Two light beers are my upper limit, and during a tournament it's one.

How to Cheat

There is something known as scientific cheating—knowing which foods to cheat with and which foods to avoid so that you may vary the meals without destroying the diet. Here is a list, from the most desirable to cheat with to the least desirable.

1. Sugar
2. Salt
3. Excess protein
4. Fat
5. Cholesterol
6. Excess kilocalories

This list may be surprising. Most people think that sugar is the most harmful part of a diet, but in Robert's diet it's the least. Sugar is empty calories, but it does supply energy. So, if you cheat, it's best to cheat on sugar.

As for salt, Americans consume far too much sodium. It is everywhere, in processed foods, fast foods, almost everything. For this reason I do not use a salt shaker when I eat, and it has cut my salt consumption in half. Since following this rule, my blood pressure has gone down.

Too much protein, as I've stated, is harmful, and as for fat, avoid it at all times unless you are training very rigorously.

Cholesterol is the most important to stay away from because the body cannot metabolize or burn cholesterol for calories. It remains in your system until excreted or until it deposits itself on your arteries. Though cholesterol is essential for life, you do not have to eat it because your body makes plenty of it. I was quite a bit above my proper cholesterol level, but these days my blood is very clean—as clean as an eight-year-old's.

Apart from the benefits already mentioned about this way of eating, my diet can improve sleeping patterns, promote a loss of body fat, and help relieve monthly cramping. I have never had any trouble sleeping, but I was happily surprised by my weight loss, and my body fat is down to 10 percent, which is very low in female athletes. Most female athletes are at about 15 percent, and the general population in America has 24 to 28 percent body fat. With my monthly period this diet is great. I am so much more on an even keel now. I never feel out of it, as I used to. I get no cramps before my period and a lighter blood flow during my menstrual cycle. My reflexes used to leave me, but not anymore, and I'm not crabby and irritable, as I used to be a few days before. This is very important, because at least half of my losses in any year were one or two days before my period.

This program has totally changed my outlook on eating, and it has even affected my tastes. I used to love greasy foods and eat them all the time, which was okay because my stomach was built to take it. Now I find myself taking the skin off chicken and cutting away the fried parts of foods. I used to love pasta only with butter and cheese, but now I like a light tomato sauce with it. I have learned how to talk to waiters and ask them how things are prepared. It is sometimes hard to hear them describe something delicious and then have to say, "Hold the sauce" or "Leave off the butter," but when I see the results, it's worth it. And Robert has allowed me to indulge in my favorite foods every once in a while. I love cream sauces and whipped cream, Peking duck and spareribs, crepes suzette and ice cream. If I win a tournament I allow myself one deviation, but I don't pig out. I never eat too much of anything.

Here's a sample day's food:

Breakfast. Pancakes or waffles, or perhaps oatmeal. For a sweetener I use Equal, which has become sort of the official sweetener of the Haas diet. I use no butter, no syrup. I will have a piece of fruit. (During the day I will snack on fruit as well.)

Lunch.   I will have a large salad with oil-free dressing, perhaps a shrimp cocktail, baked potato, or maybe spaghetti. (Probably spaghetti. I eat pasta all the time.) If I get hungry before dinner, I will have a bagel or a roll and some fruit.

Dinner.   Fish cooked without butter, a baked or sweet potato, green or yellow vegetables, a large salad, and fruit for dessert.

Beverages.   During the course of the day I will drink a lot of water, fruit and vegetable juices (fresh carrot is my favorite), Perrier and lime, and an occasional light beer.

Sometimes athletes try to lose weight right before or during an event. Wrestlers are always trying to lose weight to make their weight class, and they suffer from this practice. I do not try to lose any weight during a tournament because my maximum aerobic capacity would decline. If I need to lose weight I will wait for an off-week to do so.

Vegetarians

A vegetarian diet can be an extremely healthy one if it is followed in a scientific fashion. There are too many vegetarians who eat an excess of cheese and whole milk and who allow their cholesterol levels to climb. But for the most part, vegetarians show much better health, less obesity, and a lower mortality rate from diet-related diseases than the general population. A vegetarian athlete would do well to understand her body's needs.

Most vegetarians allow themselves some sort of milk or egg products, while others even deviate enough to eat chicken or fish. In the strictest sense this is not a vegetarian diet at all, but it can be a healthy one so long as you remember that your body requires B_{12}, which is usually derived from animal protein. You can easily get as much as you need from skim or low-fat dairy products, and those foods will also afford you minerals such as calcium and magnesium. If you are very strict about being a total vegetarian, then you absolutely must take a B_{12} supplement. This can be purchased in any health-food store.

Nutritional Supplements

It is a good idea to supplement your diet with vitamins and minerals, particularly if you are an athlete. I use some, and they are a safe, simple, and effective way of getting all the nutrients my body requires on a daily basis. Everything I take is easily obtained in a good health-food store. I recommend that you seek a sports-care professional who understands your supplementary needs and can direct you to the necessary vitamins and dosages.

Prematch Eats

I know, I know. Eating right before a match is a dumb thing to do. It makes you feel heavy and drowsy and robs the body of blood that must be used to digest the food. But personally I cannot play when I am the slightest bit hungry. This can pose a big problem to me when my match is held up by rain delays or if there is an unusually long match before mine that I hadn't counted on. This makes it difficult to calculate when I should eat. So it is not unusual for me to be snacking right up until the time I play. I don't try to put down burgers and shakes, mind you. It's usually a piece of fruit, a slice of bread, a cookie—anything to fill me up quickly and stay with me for a while. As a matter of fact, I have been seen on more than one occasion actually munching away on something during changeovers, especially during doubles matches. By then I am already into my fourth hour of match play, and I want to make sure I don't run out of gas out there.

Injuries

My personal case history of injuries reads lighter than those of many of my peers. I have had a few minor aches nag me from time to time, but my worst and most consistent injuries have been to my shoulder. I originally aggravated it back in 1975, when I felt a little soreness after one of my early-round matches. I went to a really careless doctor, who promptly gave me a cortisone injection to stop the pain. Well, I couldn't even raise my arm the next day, so he shot me again and again. I made it through my semifinal match but was forced to default the finals to Chrissie Evert, something I had never done before. I felt terrible about it, but even worse, I needed four weeks of rest to recover. After that I had a full year of painless play, but then the condition returned, and it had grown more complicated. Large calcium deposits had formed inside my shoulder and were not disintegrating by themselves. The doctor who explained this to me threw in his answer to the problem: shoulder operation. "Thanks," I said, "but I'll be going now." There was no way that I wanted to get cut for this—there just had to be another solution. In the meantime, the pain was excruciating. It was so bad that I couldn't drive my backhand at all, and one match got so bad that I played my opponent, Sue Barker, using an improvised two-handed backhand. To relieve the pressure on the shoulder I then had the brainstorm of using my wrist more and my shoulder less. The result: a wrist so sore that it required cortisone as well. This is getting ridiculous, I thought. To add insult to injury, I sprained my ankle stepping on a football and hopped around on crutches for two glorious weeks. I was a walking injury festival.

In 1978 I sought out the late Dr. John Marshall, the doctor who had helped Billie Jean King so much with her knees. He gave me the proper injections to dissolve the calcium buildup and put me on a weight-training program that strengthened my entire upper body. For the past four years I can honestly say that I have had no serious injuries. There is a tendency for me to get tightness in the lower region of my back, so I take special care with that, doing plenty of slow stretching to warm it up. I ice my shoulder after each match and use heat when needed on my back, also after matches. On grass courts, where I tend to dive and flail at the ball a lot, I take extra care to arrive warm. I have become extremely conscientious of the proper care of my body and the ways to prevent injury.

Children's Injuries

When I was a kid I used to roll out of bed and start serving, and to a certain extent I got away with it. All I can say is, I was lucky. It is just as important for kids to stretch and prepare as it is for adults. Why learn your lessons the painful way? Look what happened to Tracy Austin, who has been plagued with back problems for more than two years. Tracy's injury made the rest of us focus on our own bodies, and the trainers on tour with us have drummed into our heads the importance of stretching, icing, taping, and pacing ourselves in order to prevent injury.

There are plenty of young players on the tour who overplay. They practice for hours on end, even on match days, and then wonder why their knee is feeling sore and their shoulder hurts at night. If you maintain too heavy a playing schedule, casualties will be a foregone conclusion. Understand your body well enough to know when it's time to get off the court.

Today, kids hit the ball much harder than I did at fourteen, fifteen, and sixteen. Much harder. And at those ages they are already playing in adult events, where they are forced to up their pace to survive. This trend is a big mistake. I always stuck pretty much to my own age group throughout my childhood years. Everyone did, really. It was much healthier that way.

Sometimes it's not even the young player's idea. There are too many mothers and fathers who are living their lives through their children. They see the money and the fame, and they relish the prospect of becoming somebody. Overzealous parents have demanded so much from their kids that they have ended up with burnouts and head cases instead of champions. I have watched plenty of them get blinded and totally lose their perspective of the game. It would be a lot nicer and certainly a lot healthier if there were more parents like Colette Evert, Chris's mom. She has never lost sight of what is important. There are many more parents who have.

If you are young and want to dedicate yourself to tennis, keep in mind that you will be putting an awful lot of stress and strain on still-growing bones, and a lot of heavy-duty practicing will truly tax your body. You may be young, but you are not invincible. If this is to become something serious with you, train seriously, sensibly, and consistently.

Injury Prevention for Kids

Here are some good rules for youngsters to remember about training.

Do not overdo it.   Make sure that you do not try to exceed your own personal limit. Do not invite unfair comparisons when you train. Listen carefully to everything that your body tells you. You know what it is saying better than anyone. You want to do battle against other players, not yourself. Stay in tune with your own body's needs, no matter what the other player is feeling.

Enjoy your youth.   I really mean it. This is your childhood, your growing time. Do not be in any rush to grow up fast, either physically or emotionally. You shouldn't try to take on adult-sized pressures, responsibilities, work loads, or goals. Wait until you are better equipped. Wait until you are older.

Take care of physical maladies immediately. If you've got a bruise, a sore spot, a strain, or any kind of muscle pull, attend to it right away. This idea of "playing through the pain" is for the birds. If you suspect that something might be serious, do not hesitate to see a doctor about it. You get issued only one body. Don't gamble it away.

When to Use Ice, When to Use Heat

In the event of muscle pulls, strains, or contusions (bruises), ice should be applied immediately. Ice anesthetizes the injured area and decreases circulation so that there isn't as much internal bleeding. Ice will also decrease the amount of scar tissue that will build up within the injured area, and by reducing swelling, ice gives you more mobility and a quicker recovery. Sometimes you should ice even before you go to play tennis. If a joint is hot it means that there is some acute inflammation going on inside. Icing for a few minutes will relieve the pain and inflammation.

There is such a thing as overicing an injury, which makes the entire procedure counterproductive. If you are using ice to decrease internal bleeding, take the ice off when the area feels cold. At that point you have forced the blood vessels to constrict in an effort to conserve heat. If you leave the ice on for too long, the body will respond by dilating the blood vessels (opening them up), and you will get too much blood to the injured area. It is your body's way of trying to warm up from the cold you have subjected it to. Remove ice if you reach the point where your skin stings or burns.

Applying external heat, such as a heating pad, to the body is a very tricky maneuver. Heat increases circulation and accelerates blood, so it is used sometimes on the back area and by arthritis patients. A heat pack may feel good, but the heat really only goes about a quarter of an inch into your skin and has no anesthetic affect whatever. The best way to increase heat in your muscles is to get a sweat going. If you start playing after having worked up a sweat, you have achieved what a heating pad would have done—you have gotten the blood pumping. This kind of internal heating is the safest way to get warm. Overheating can cause second- and third-degree burns to the skin.

Tennis Injuries and Their Treatment

Tennis Elbow

Tennis elbow can be caused by overuse, an improper stroke, or a weakness in the shoulder area. The shoulder is the initiator and stabilizer of force and motion in your stroke. If for some reason—an improper swing or a repeatedly late contact point—your shoulder is being used incorrectly and stress is being put on your wrist and elbow, you're going to feel it. The first thing to do is to correct the stroke if it is faulty. Then build up strength in your elbow and shoulder, especially your shoulder. If you require rest, take it. Ice continually, especially after you play for any length of time. If the pain persists, consult a doctor, who may want to use ultrasound treatment or suggest a brace.

Pulled Hamstring and Groin Muscles

If you have pulled or strained these parts of your body, you must build strength back into the area. Otherwise, what's left will only get weaker and more severely injured. Pulled hamstring and groin muscles must be made more flexible as well as strong, so you must work in unison and moderation to achieve both. Rest and ice the injury, then use weights to strengthen the area slowly. After training, stretch the muscle, making sure not to jerk and bounce. Do not exceed your limits while you are injured, such as flying after balls that you have no business going for. The worst part about these types of injuries is that they can become chronic if not treated correctly. Exercise common sense along with everything else.

Knee Injuries

Be extremely careful with knee injuries. The knee has a very bony architecture. It is the largest joint in the body, an intricate system of tendons, muscles, and ligaments. The same system that gives the knee stability is responsible for its flexibility, so a weak or injured knee can give you all kinds of headaches. Ice a knee immediately after an injury, and if swelling does not go down or the knee gives out on you, consult a doctor. Strengthen the knee with weights, especially concentrating on building the quadriceps and other surrounding muscles. But what is important to remember is that weight training should be done under strict supervision. It is possible to develop certain sets of muscles while ignoring others, and this imbalance can cause severe tears and pulls in the neglected regions.

Eye Injuries

If you should get hit in the eye with a ball, ice the eye immediately. Then check all the eye movements to make sure that the eye is working properly—side to side, up and down—and that your vision has not been impaired. If you have spots, blurring, or double vision, see a doctor immediately. Otherwise, be certain that the tear ducts work, you've got a good response to light, there is no bleeding, and the eyelid can close normally. If you start to have headaches, see your doctor.

Ankle Injuries

If you twist, turn, or sprain your ankle, get off your feet immediately and ice, elevate, and compress the ankle with an Ace bandage to stop the swelling. If you heard something snap or pop, see your doctor.

Back Injuries

Back injuries are common if you play when tired, if you've got an unusual service motion, or if your legs are insufficiently warmed up and not moving correctly. If your hamstring or quadricep muscles or hips are tight, the back has to take on the rotation duties of your hips, and this can cause severe stress and debilitation. Make sure that you do not overwork your back. If you do, check your form, rest, and see a doctor. Be very cautious here, because bad backs don't go away.

Types of Rest

When I first began playing on the women's pro tour in 1973, I played just about every tournament there was, week after week, month after month. When it became apparent that I needed a rest from the game, I'd take a few weeks off and make a clean break, a total departure. This meant that I not only stopped playing tennis, I stopped being physically active altogether. It was the worst. I'd lounge around the house, sit in the sunlight, or pig out in front of the television set. I'd wind up needing more of a rest from my rest than my tournament weeks, because I'd have fallen apart within five days. The first thing that would go would always be my legs, but my lethargy took a mental toll as well, so that instead of coming back eager and refreshed from my vacation, I'd be dancing madly backward, trying to regain lost ground. Some rest that turned out to be.

These days I play a lot fewer tournaments and win a lot more titles. Renee and Nancy have helped me to use my rests to make me stronger and more dedicated than ever before. On some rest weeks, the last thing I do is take a rest from tennis. I may take a week or two off before the European clay court season begins so that Renee and I can switch my game from the slick green carpet courts of the winter to the slow red clay of the summer. During those kinds of "rest" weeks, I play about five hours of tennis a day. I will also do my weight training and running drills and play a lot of basketball during these periods of practice, and it's during these weeks that I put in the most amount of work on improving my game.

I have another type of rest week—the type I need when I am really tennised out or a little bit tired or perhaps slightly injured. I will put away my tennis racket—stick it in the closet with a "Do Not Touch" sign on it. I get tennis out of my mind. Actually, I can get it out only about 99.9 percent, but for me that's pretty good. I will not think about my game, my schedule, my ranking, and I skip the tennis results in the sports pages. I catch up on the activities of my friends, write letters, go to movies. But I am always an athlete and I never lose my need for competition and stimulation. I used to play a lot of golf, and I still hit the greens quite a bit, but more than anything, I play basketball. For me basketball has become the great escape from tennis. Nancy has taught me a lot about her game, and when we go one on one or set up a game with others, it's as exhausting and exhilarating as any tennis match. Basketball complements tennis in so many ways that I cannot recommend the game highly enough. It builds up the cardiovascular system, quickens reflexes, improves foot speed, and, believe me, I have never jumped higher for my overheads than I do now, after months of leaping around the basketball court. When I come off a rest week like this, my competitive instincts are just as keen as they were when I left, my head is clear, my spirit eager. It only takes a day or two of practice with the racket before I rejoin the tour, anxious to play the next match.

My advice is to pace yourself. When you are in need of a break, for whatever reason, take it. If you need work on your game, devote your rest time to the problems. If your game is physically sound but you are suffering from mental fatigue and low confidence, put a little distance between yourself and the game for a while. You will know what your needs are more than anyone, so listen carefully to yourself. Whatever kind of rest you take, make sure not to lose your desire, eagerness, and instincts for the game. Those, after all, are what a break is for.

The Tennis Basics

Footwork

Everything you do in sports begins in your legs. From your lower body you draw your strength, speed, balance, and center of gravity. Footwork is generally the most overlooked aspect of tennis. Far too much emphasis is placed on hitting the ball, but making contact with the ball is just about the simplest thing you do in the sport. Moreover, in the course of a two-set match the total hitting time is only a few minutes. It is everything that has gone on before you make contact that determines how good a shot you are going to get off. Therefore, your footwork is actually the key. There is not a single top-ranked player in the world who does not move to the ball exceptionally well, simply because it is impossible to be a top player if you have poor movement. The majority of errors made in tennis are direct results of poor movement, which is why I cannot stress footwork enough.

I am one of the fastest players on the tour, but my footwork is probably the weakest part of my game. Fortunately for me, I have always been strong enough and talented enough to hide a lot of faulty footwork.

I have hit plenty of late balls and have still gotten off clean shots, an option most people are not given. But being constantly slow to the ball greatly reduces options, making those players easier to figure out. The fact that imparting topspin requires much more time than imparting slice on a ball kept me from being able to produce topspin off my backhand for many years. My running forehand is a shot that I still rely on too often. While the shot is a real crowd-pleaser, flashy and dramatic to the galleries, it is a low-percentage way to do business. So now I am sighting the ball earlier, taking quicker steps, and really getting behind the ball, and I've become a far more dangerous opponent than I ever was.

By improving your footwork, you will automatically improve other aspects of your game. First, you will improve your control. The earlier you get to the ball, the more time you give yourself to prepare your shot, get behind the ball, and put a good finish on the stroke. Good footwork will also improve your power. When you are forced to play balls on the run, you lose most of the power in your legs, back, and shoulders, and all you are really left with are the muscles in your arm. Move quickly enough so that you can transfer all of your body weight forward and into the ball.

You can also improve your disguise. Chris Evert Lloyd is tough to play against because by moving so well to the ball she can prepare every stroke to look exactly the same. Because of this immaculate preparation her opponents cannot make a move to the ball until the very moment when Chris makes contact. Slower players are often left with few options to play and force themselves into defensive positions, where they can only lob or play to one area of the court, or only use one spin on the ball. The earlier you get to the ball, the more ways you can hit it.

Your court positioning will also improve with good footwork. Once you fall a little behind just one ball in a rally you diminish your ability to cover the rest of the shots. It is a very cagey player who can recover court positioning in the middle of a rally, and it is usually a surprise attack or a well-placed lob that gets them back into the point. The quicker you are, the more in control of the court you become, and the better your chances of dictating the point.

By being able to move quickly to the ball, your ability to pressure opponents will improve, since your opponent will be forced to rush her shot. You always want to gain time for yourself, and in doing so you will take time away from the player on the other side of the court. It can be a very intimidating thing to look up from a shot you've just hit and see your opponent already jumping on top of it. Even if you feel as though you don't have a chance on a ball, make the effort anyway. If your opponent passes you at the net cleanly, without any kind of fight, her confidence will grow. But if you read the shot early and make a go of it, even a failed effort can intimidate your opponent. She will say to herself, "Boy, that was my best shot, and she *still* got close to it!" She may try to do too much with the ball the next time and miss the mark. So run everything down. Your opponent will start asking herself what it takes to win a point against you, and that kind of pressure might win you the match. Make her hit that one extra shot.

Footwork and Racketwork

Remember that as you run to the ball, your racket should immediately move into the proper hitting position. Your racketwork must blend perfectly with your footwork or your shot will be inefficient.

You may think that you can run your fastest with your arms pumping at your sides, but this is not the case on the tennis court. You must get comfortable running with your racket head poised to hit so that you are not pinched and hurried at the moment of impact, or flailing uselessly after a ball that has escaped behind your strings. With enough practice and concentration this will become automatic to you. I guarantee that your shots will improve considerably.

How to Hold the Racket

The most important thing about gripping the racket is that you be aware at all times of where your racket face is in relation to your body and the oncoming ball. As long as you are able to produce your strokes with the grips you use, you are okay. But if you are using a bizarre grip that is limiting your options on any ball, you must make a change. I have been tinkering with my grips all my life, and in recent years Renee Richards has adjusted the grips on nearly all of my shots to allow for more topspin on my groundstrokes, more feel on my touch shots, and more slice on my serves. The biggest change is on my forehand side. I'd always had a really snappy cross-court forehand, but Renee explained to me that the grip I'd been using was prohibiting me from developing a true and lethal topspin on that side. I had to make a radical change on my grip, and it felt funny for a long time. I thought I'd never see my beloved cross-court forehand again. But the change was most definitely for the better, and now I am fluent in every spin and pace off my forehand side. Owning the proper grip can be vital to the growth and maturation of your game. Don't lock yourself into a limited style of play just because you don't want to change your grip. The bother can really be worth it.

The Continental Grip

The Continental is my basic forehand grip, and most of my other strokes are also hit with a variation of the Continental grip. Roy Emerson taught me the simplest way to find the Continental grip. Simply slide your palm flat along the strings of your racket, straight down until you reach the handle of the racket. If I want more topspin on my forehand I will move my palm over toward a more Western grip (see p. 61) so that I have more hand on the racket and thereby hit a heavier ball. When I am slicing my forehand for an approach shot I will again adjust my grip slightly, moving my hand more toward an Eastern grip (see p. 60). This allows for a more open racket face. Conversely, my backhand slice is more Continental than Eastern to allow for the same open racket face at the moment of contact.

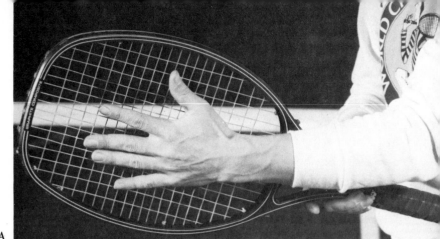

11A

11B

11C

Fig. 11 *The Continental Grip*

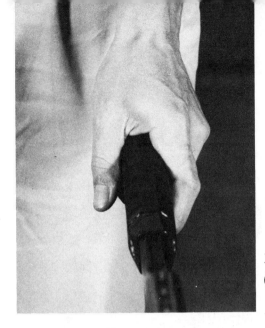

11D
(aerial view)

The Eastern Grip

The Eastern is my basic backhand grip and the one I use for most of my serves. To find this grip, lay the racket vertically on the court and pick it up, hammerstyle, straight from the top of the handle. For extra topspin on my backhand and extra spin on my serve, I adjust the grip slightly to make for an even more profound Eastern grip. On my kick serves and for my flat serve I will move my hand back over toward the Continental forehand grip.

The Western Grip

The Western grip is the least used of the three. While it is excellent in dealing with high shots and for imparting topspin, it is deadly to use on very low shots and volleys. To find the Western grip, simply lay the racket face down on the ground and pick it up. You now hold the Bjorn Borg grip. As I said, the only time I will use this grip is if I want to put even more topspin on my forehand than I normally would. (See p. 61.)

12A

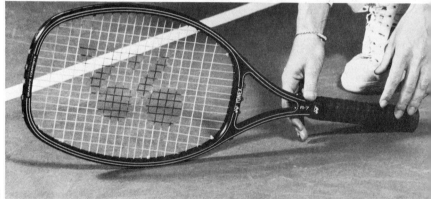

12B

12C

Fig. 12 *The Eastern Grip*

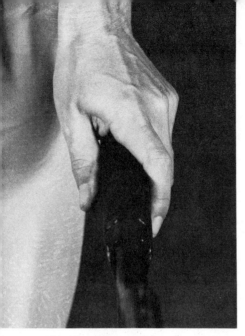

12D *(aerial view)*

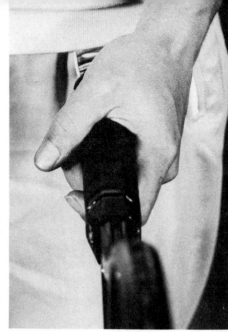

Fig. 13 *The Western Grip*

The Forehand

The Topspin Forehand

As the ball approaches you, drop your racket head down below your waist so that you will be stroking from below the ball. The racket face is slightly closed and the wrist is rather loose, but only from up to down, not twisting side to side. Meet the ball early and out in front of your lead foot. Your weight is transferred forward at this moment so that you make full use of your body power. With your eye fixed on the ball, brush over the top of it, completing the low-to-high swing. After contact the follow-through should be long and smooth. Be sure to hit the topspin forehand from 6 to 12 o'clock. Keep the elbow close to the body and get close to the ball. Stay behind it. Keep the ball in front, and don't overrun it.

14A

14B

14D

14E

Fig. 14 *The topspin forehand*

14C

The Slice Forehand

The slice forehand is used primarily as an approach shot or to counter a high bouncing ball and must also be hit as a last measure when you have no time for a drive. I sometimes use a slice if I suddenly want to quicken the pace of the rally and catch my opponent off guard. As the ball approaches you, turn your shoulders and bring the racket back above the level of the ball. The racket head should tilt upward above the wrist, and the wrist should be very firm. Transfer your weight forward, and meet the ball in front with a slightly open racket face. Continue the swing in the

15A

15B

15D

Fig. 15 *The slice forehand*

15E

15C

direction of your target and keep the follow-through short and sweet.

The Flat Forehand

The flat forehand is a virtual block of the ball. Use a very firm wrist and a compact backswing. The face of the racket is wide open. Make contact well in front of your body and keep the follow-through long and smooth.

16A

16B

16D

Fig. 16 *The flat forehand*

16E

16C

The Backhand

The Topspin Backhand

I find it much harder to get topspin off my backhand side than my forehand side, perhaps because topspin backhands require better footwork than the open-stanced forehands that I can sometimes get away with. On all backhands the ideal point of impact is slightly more in front of the body than on a forehand.

Renee Richards gave me my topspin backhand, and when I first learned it, it was very mechanical and not at all like the great looping topspin backhand of Bettina Bunge. But finally, after a year and a half of practice, Renee told me, "I think you're ready for the loop."

17A   17B

Fig. 17 *The topspin backhand*

I mention this because hitting a topspin backhand takes
a lot of practice, but when hit right, there's not another
stroke like it.

As the ball approaches, your shoulder turns, bringing your racket back into position. Make sure that your
racket is below the level of the ball. Use your free
hand to draw the racket back smoothly—it will give
you more control and will make you aware of the face
of the racket. Shift your body weight forward as you
prepare to make contact, and meet the ball in front of
your body. Brush up and over on the ball, and as it becomes more comfortable, whip through the stroke for
momentum and power. The follow-through is long and
high.

17C

17D   17E

18A   18B

Fig. 18 *The slice backhand*

Also, turn the shoulders, and bend the elbow on the backswing, not with a straight arm. The elbow and racket should be down under the ball. Hit from 6 to 12 o'clock with top spin. Don't let the ball get behind you.

The Slice Backhand

This is one of my best shots and one that I often follow to the net. The slice backhand is a good on-the-run shot because it is neat and compact and naturally leans you into the court. As the ball approaches, pivot and draw your racket back above the level of the ball. Keep a stiff wrist and point the racket head above it. Bite into the ball from high to low with a slightly open racket

18C

18D

18E

19A   19B

Fig. 19 *The flat backhand*

face, and make contact slightly in front of your body.
The follow-through is short and snappy but should stay
smooth. It is a common mistake to pull off this shot too
early.

The Flat Backhand

You need a very strong wrist and arm to produce a flat
backhand because the backswing is minimal. This is a
blocked stroke, just like the flat forehand, and, again,
be sure to make contact well in front of your body or the
ball will buzz into your strings and you will hit the ball
hopelessly wide. The follow-through is long and smooth,
just like on the forehand side.

19C

19D

19E

Two-handed Backhand

Until I was nine years old I used a two-handed back-hand, and I was told to give it up because the stroke was inhibiting my reach. There are both advantages and disadvantages to owning a two-handed backhand. The biggest disadvantage is, in fact, its lack of reach, so if you wish to use both hands, make sure that you are fast enough to overcome this drawback. There are plenty of pluses to owning a two-handed backhand. If you are naturally weak on that side, both hands on the racket will greatly improve your strength. Using both hands gives you great racket head control and makes disguis-ing your intentions easy. You have the advantage of waiting until the very last moment to decide where you want to hit the ball—a real plus for passing shots. The things to remember about two-handed shots are these:

1. You must be very quick to the ball because you have limited reach.
2. You do not have the long follow-through of a one-handed backhand, so be sure to get your racket back early for better control.
3. Allow the ball to come a little bit closer to your body than if you were a one-handed backhand player so that you keep the rotation of both your shoulders in a powerful hitting area.
4. Keep both hands on the racket even after contact with the ball for more control and smoothness.

Groundstrokes

There are several things you must remember about hit-ting groundstrokes. The first is that groundstrokes are the most fundamental part of the game, so both your forehand and backhand must be sound.

Early preparation is the key to good groundstrokes. At the very moment that your opponent makes contact with the ball, you should prepare your reply. The response must be immediate and without extraneous movements. While waiting for a shot, your body should be forward into the court, knees flexed, waist slightly bent, weight on the balls of your feet, and eyes trained on the ball. Your racket should be in front of your body in a neutral ready position so that you may turn to the forehand or the backhand with equal ease.

Keep your strokes simple. Pivot sideways to the net, keep your center of gravity low throughout your swing, and meet the ball in front of your body. The ideal point of contact for a groundstroke is at waist height, and you should accommodate this height as much as possible to ensure repetition of the stroke. On a low bouncing ball, bend to the ball and make the stroke from a lower hitting position. Bend from the waist as well as from the knees. On high balls, step back, then into the shot.

Always be aware of the angle of the racket face on groundstrokes. This has much to do with the outcome of the stroke. Do not take your eyes off the ball until after it has left your racket strings. Focus in again as your opponent makes her shot.

If your contact point is too late you will be forced to hit down the line because the arm is cramped in its swing. Keep all of your options open by hitting an early ball. The earlier you meet the ball, the sharper you are able to hit cross-court. Avoid hitting groundstrokes on the run. Off-balance shots lack control and power. Do not overrun the ball. By getting too close you will inhibit your natural swing and end up with a cramped shot.

Practice hard to develop good depth on both swings and multiple spins. Last, make certain that you finish the stroke. The follow-through on groundstrokes helps to control them.

Footwork on Groundstrokes

The first few steps to the ball should be long and explosive. React right off the strings of your opponent and take off. Once you are in motion, your steps should become shorter but remain very rapid so that you can judge the exact position you should be in for your reply. You want to be behind every single ball, and although this is not always possible, it is what you should shoot for. A common mistake people make is that they produce one shot, then stand in the same place and wait for the next ball. Run right back into the proper position off each groundstroke you hit. Any delay will make you late to the next ball.

For years I would adjust my footwork according to the pace of the ball hit to me. What an error that is! I would think that I had all of this free time on my hands to mosey over to the ball, but what I was doing was letting my opponent get away with a weak shot and, at the same time, cutting down my own options on the ball. If you are given a slow ball to play, do not slow down your footwork. Attack!

Hitting High Groundstrokes

If I am hit a high backhand I know I will not be able to produce a lot of power, I will take the ball on the rise and slice it cross-court. On backhands I prefer to go for an angle rather than trying to hit a good length on the shot, because of my limited strength up there. However, on a high forehand I nearly always go for length, both down the line and cross-court. If the ball is high and short on either side I will play it flat, hitting right down into my opponent's court.

Hitting Low Groundstrokes

If the groundstroke is hit low, then that's where I've got to be to reply to it, so I bend more from my waist and put extra flex in my knees. A nice low bounce, if it's not the skidding kind, as on grass courts, is ideal for topspin, especially if the shot was designed for use as an approach shot, because then my topspin groundstrokes will be tougher for the oncoming net player to volley. If the ball is bouncing extremely low—so much so that I cannot get under it—I will slice or hit flat and cross-court where the net clearance is lower and my percentages are higher.

Spins for Groundstrokes

Topspin

The beauty of topspin on groundstrokes is that it allows you to hit the ball with more control and pace and greater depth. Topspin causes the ball to turn toward your opponent and into the court. The ball dips downward, which makes topspin my favorite passing-shot spin, since it forces my opponent to hit up on the volley. Topspin is safer to hit than the other spins because the ball clears the net by a lot, allowing for a great margin of error. Topspin takes more time to prepare for than the other spins, so if you wish to add topspin to your game, be sure that you are speedy enough to do so.

The biggest mistake people make in trying to achieve topspin is in using their wrist and flicking over the ball. The wrist should not twist and turn on a topspin shot; it should go from down to up, just like the rest of the arm. But the first thing to do is to close the face of your racket, anywhere from 45 to 60 degrees, depending on how much spin you wish to impart to the ball. Your wrist should really be loose so that you can whip through the ball at the moment of contact. Stay low, and maintain a low center of gravity throughout the shot. By pulling up from your shot too early you will lose the work on the ball. Although every player has a different backswing, my best advice is to draw the racket back simply and very low to the ground. If you use a looping motion or draw your racket back high, for topspin make sure that the racket gets under the ball right from the start of the motion. Your swing should travel from low to high, the racket face should be closed throughout, and contact should be made in front of your body. Get close to the ball and hit it from 6 to 12 o'clock, keeping the elbow close to the body. Get behind the ball and keep the ball in front. Don't overrun it.

Slice Spin

The slice is a more defensive spin by nature because it carries less speed than a topspin or flat ball. But the slice spin is a very necessary part of anyone's game, especially a serve-and-volley player's. Because the slice is a shorter stroke than the topspin and takes less preparation time, it is the ideal approach-shot spin, it allows for the surprise shots such as lobs and drop shots, it can suddenly change the pace of a rally, and it offers a lot of control.

The slice is basically a short, chopping stroke hit with a firm wrist. Its backswing is a little longer than a volley's and so is its follow-through, but everything else about it is much the same. Take your racket back high, the racket face open to about 45 degrees. Turn your shoulders and swing down toward the ball, meeting it slightly out in front of your body. Do not merely chop at the ball and quit on the stroke at the point of contact. Finish the swing up high and out toward the direction of your target.

Flat Spin

It's pretty hard to hit a totally flat ball, a ball with no spin on it at all, and there are very few top players who would risk hitting flat shots with any kind of regularity because it is such a low-percentage way to hit the ball. Jimmy Connors hits flatter than anyone, and the penetration he gets on his shots is awesome. The only times to hit the ball flat is when you are blocking a flat ball hit at you and have no time for another spin, or when the ball is high enough over the net for you to hit directly down into your opponent's court. There is very little backswing involved. The idea is to block the ball back, so you must keep a firm wrist, meet the ball out in front of your body, and be sure to transfer your weight forward just before impact. Follow through on the stroke or your ball will bazooka its way into the next county.

How to Use Spins on Groundstrokes

The amount of time your opponent has afforded you to hit your groundstroke is key to the spin you place on the ball. If your opponent's shot is very flat and deep, your only reply is to counter with a flat ball, or perhaps a lob. You will have little time to impart any sort of effective spin, so just block the ball back. If the approaching ball is a short and high sitter, barely clearing the net, attack also with a flat shot. Take the ball early and hammer it away for a winner. The only other time to hit a flat ball is when you are given a shot that bounces at just the right height for a flat smack—a bounce between the knees and lower ribs. That height is the only comfortable place really to tag the fuzz. If the ball bounces above your ribs, go to a slice. Below that, use slice or topspin. On medium-paced shots, again, the choice of spins is yours.

My best advice for groundstroke spins is to go with the spin. By that I mean you should not try to counter topspin with topspin and slice with slice. Trying to reply to a topspin ball with even more topspin of your own means that you must abolish all the work on your opponent's ball, then produce equal topspin of your own. You would have to stand back and whale at the ball to do this. By slicing instead, you are taking the original pace of the ball and merely changing its direction. The slice is far easier to produce, and you can make contact from much farther into the court. This is also true of a ball sliced at you. To slice back would mean imparting the opposite spin to the ball, so go over it instead. The heavier the slice, the more you should topspin, and vice versa. If your opponent mixes up her spins, so should you. Sylvia Hanika of Germany has some of the best spins in women's tennis—both topspin and slice. For every topspin that she hits to me I will slice her, and for every slice I will come over the ball. I always want to use what I have been given. I'll take what I get and go with it.

Groundstroke Drills

In order to groove your strokes, constant repetition is necessary. One drill is for two players to hit to each other down the lines and cross-court, but players shouldn't overdo this kind of drilling, because it is unrealistic. Never in a match will you and your opponent feed each other the same stroke over and over again. A variation of this drill is far superior. One of you hits nothing but cross-court shots while the other hits nothing but down-the-liners. This will keep both of you running all over the court while stressing your groundstrokes as well. Switch around, and if you are in very good shape, one of you can stand at net while the other is on the baseline—much tougher for both players because the time is cut severely between shots.

All forms of two-on-one drills are good if they stress depth, pace, and control. Two at the net playing one on the baseline is tough for the solitary groundstroker, and so is the two-on-one drill when there are two baseliners against one. Play these games to 11 points and then switch positions so that everyone has a chance alone.

The Volley

I had a photograph of Billie Jean King hitting a forehand volley, which Renee tacked on my wall. It was a great photo—Billie with knees bent, her left one very nearly touching the ground, a perfectly balanced body, and her racket out in front of her face, eyes looking right through the strings. I studied this photo because I like to play the net as much as Billie Jean does. It is there that I am most comfortable and at my most aggressive. Coming to the net robs my opponent of time and gives me much more angle into my opponent's court, so the net is my ultimate goal and the volley my golden weapon.

Except for a reverse in footwork, the mechanics of the forehand and backhand volley are the same. Both should be hit with a slight backhand grip. I am a believer in keeping things economical and sound, especially at the net. In fact, the credo of the volleying game is "Keep it short and simple." Your knees should be bent, legs comfortably apart, and body weight forward. Your wrist must be very firm, since a ball will be buzzing into your racket at any moment. Your elbow should be closely tucked into your body, and as you pick up the direction of your opponent's ball, pivot your shoulder. Your leading shoulder will create a leading foot as well, and at this point you are turned sideways to the net.

20A

20B

Fig. 20 *The forehand volley*

20C

The turn you make with your shoulder is the extent of your backswing. Your racket should never fade any farther behind your body than that, and the racket face should be open as if hitting a slice. The power you achieve comes not from a swing but from your opponent's pace, your firm wrist, good timing, and transferring your body weight forward. Hit the ball out in front of you and try to catch it at its highest point over the net. The finish is firm and lacks any kind of follow-through. The only time when there is any swing on the volley is when your opponent's ball is softly hit and you must put something on it to drive it better into the court. This is known as a swing volley. But usually when you come to the net your opponent hits the ball even harder than she originally intended.

Footwork on the Volley

When you are at the net you have no time for intricate little steps to the ball. At the net you have just enough time for one or two long strides—a forward lunging effort, if you will. Your shoulders should work in syncopation with your feet, and both your lead foot and your shoulder should turn automatically into the direction of the oncoming ball. The most common error players make is taking little stutter steps that do absolutely no good at all. This is no time to tap dance, since there's a ball headed right at you. Take a long crossover step right away and follow that with whatever other steps are necessary to get to the ball. Turn the shoulders, and hit the ball with a firm wrist and no backswing.

Hitting High Volleys

I usually play high volleys flat on either side, although the high backhand volley will have some slice on it. If I am volleying cross-court I will play an acute angle off the court. If I am volleying down the line, I will go for depth. It is difficult to get a lot of power from up there, especially on the backhand side, so I lock my wrist and try to lean my body weight into the shot.

Hitting Low Volleys

On low volleys I get down very nearly to my knees and hold the racket with an extra-firm grip. I open up the face of the racket just slightly for added height, and more often than not I hit cross-court, either very deeply or very deftly. A very quiet drop volley can be a nice little reply here. Generally on low shots, ground-strokes, or volleys you should hit cross-court because the net is quite a bit lower in the middle than on the sideline, so you can hit the ball harder and get a good angle as well.

Volley Drills

One of my favorite volley drills was taught to me by Roy Emerson during World Team Tennis with the Boston Lobsters. Roy wanted me to cut back my swing and hit with a firm grip as well, so he would get me to pull back off my shot at the very moment of impact. Right after I hit my volleys I would recoil from each, and this simple trick firmed up my arms like nothing else could. It cut down my follow-through so much that when I would go back to my normal stroke, it would be much more compact and crisp.

Two-on-one drills are very good for volleys. One person is up at the net against two people at the baseline, and the net player tries to defend her turf against them both. Two-on-one quick volleys are also terrific and will speed up your reflexes. A good way to practice control on your volleys is to volley into the corners, both from a stationary position and on the move. A good control drill has both players at the net—you hit your volleys cross-court at your opponent, and she returns them down the line right back at you. Then switch the pattern. You'll be amazed at how proficient you can become at this. You should also practice volley drills that require forward movement—approaching on a short ball and closing in quickly, and having your partner feed you balls that require a lot of forward movement. This drill will remind you not to let the ball dip below the level of the net and, therefore, to be more aggressive.

Because you may have to volley from midcourt on in, be sure to practice hitting from the various parts of the short court. You may not always be the ideal six feet from the net in a match, so get used to volleying from different lengths in practice. Have your practice partner stand on one side of the court and drag you back and forth along the forecourt with all of your replies going back to her.

The Serve

The following are the things you must remember about the tennis serve:

1. If you can hold service all through a match, you will almost never lose.

2. It is more important to develop consistency than power.

3. Do not step on or over the baseline before you make contact with the ball or you will be called for foot fault.

4. Do not play a very bad toss or it will throw off your natural swing. Let the ball bounce, and toss again. Make sure that your tosses are consistent and try to hit the ball at the top of the toss.

5. Mix up your serves, but generally try to play a lot of second serves to your opponent's weakness.

6. Many players have patterned returns of serve. Note your opponent's tendencies, and follow your serve with appropriate replies. Under pressure, players can be expected to hit their bread-and-butter return, so be on the lookout for it.

7. Every now and then, toss off your opponent's balance by serving directly at her. A serve into the body is difficult to respond to and is a good surprise tactic.

8. If you want to go for the flat serve, it's easier to aim it down the "T" than wide because of the dip in the net. The flat serve is a low-percentage serve, so use it sparingly. A good time to go for the big serve is when you're up 30–0, 40–0, or 40–15.

9. The best serve to follow into the net is a slice, because the spin will allow you sufficient time to get tightly into the net area. A kicked second serve is good for this as well.

10. In doubles, talk with your partner about where you both will be serving. The two of you may

want to discuss which serves are easier for you to poach off of, how you can mix up your serves so that your opponents are constantly facing a different spin and angle. And if you want to try a different serving tactic, tell your partner so she won't be as surprised as your opponents.

Types of Serve

There are three serves in tennis: the flat serve, the slice serve, and the kick serve. The slice is used more than any other and is the one serve that everyone must own, because it is the delivery with the highest percentage value. And to be an effective server, one must get a lot of first serves in. All three serves require the same stance, a coordinated rhythm of the arms, a controlled toss, and a good follow-through.

The Flat Serve

Stand with your lead foot (the left for a rightie, right for a leftie) at a 45-degree angle to the baseline and anywhere within five feet of the center of the court. The back foot is generally placed in a direct line with where you're hitting, perhaps slightly closed. The distribution of weight is a personal preference. Some players like their weight to be evenly distributed on both feet, while others rock back and forth for momentum. I take a slight stutter step to bring the weight on my back foot forward. Try to syncopate the motion of both your arms so that they move back and upward smoothly. The toss is made slightly in front of your body and with no spin. The toss is straight up and down, and the motion of a good toss is similar to that of changing a light bulb. The release is over your head and without a lot of flourish. That way the actual "toss" is very short and as controlled as possible. There should be no hang time or you will lose the momentum of your motion. The motion of the arms is as simple as possible—no funky twisting and jerking. You bend your knees as you split your arms so that you can get good spring into the ball. As you reach up, your arm should be fully extended, with the racket face hitting the ball squarely and without any spin. The momentum should carry your racket into a long and smooth follow-through toward the opponent's service court. Make sure the elbow is fully bent before uncoiling and swinging. In simplest terms, think of yourself as pawing at the ball, and liken the flat serve to the delivery of a hard ball by a baseball pitcher.

21A

21B

Fig. 21 *The flat serve*

21E

21F

21C

21D

21G

21H

Flat serve
(impact position)

The Slice Serve

The slice serve is delivered very much the same way as the flat serve, but you want to take advantage of the natural spin that your body can generate. You should not have to make a concerted effort to impart more slice on the ball if you adjust your toss and grip just slightly. If you are a right-handed player, toss the ball more to your right so that you brush the side of the ball upon contact. To gain slice even more, turn your grip so that it is an even more pronounced back-hand grip. You should twist your body, which means that you will not be making contact as far in front as you would on a flat serve. The wrist should be nice and loose and snap naturally at impact point, and the follow-through should continue past your lead leg.

The Kick Serve

This serve is also known as the topspin serve or the American twist. The toss of the kick serve is behind you, so you must sink down and bend your back to meet the ball, which is what produces the "kick." Spring up and out on this one, and connect with fearless abandon and a lot of muscle. I tend to use more of a forehand than a backhand grip on this one so that I have more hand on the handle. When I really hit this one well the kick is such that it bounces and takes off in the opposite direction of my normal spin serve. I used to hit this one a lot more when I was younger than I do now. As a matter of fact, at sixteen and seventeen I was big on hitting reverse spins on my serves and overheads, which is actually a very cocky thing even to try. But those serves, like the kick, take a lot out of my back, so I rarely go for them. Barbara Potter must have a very strong back because she hits the twist serve all the time. If you can hit this without pain, it is certainly a nice weapon in your arsenal. If you use the kick as your second serve, make sure you take a full swing and hit up on the ball; otherwise the ball will generally sail along. (See p. 96.)

22A

22B

Fig. 22 *The slice serve*

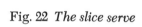

22E

22F

22C

22D

22G

22H

23A

23B

Fig. 23 *The kick serve*

23E

23F

23C

23D

23G

23H

The slice serve (impact position)   *The kick serve* (impact position)

Using the Various Spins on Serve

One of the fundamentals of effective serving is to mix up the spins, regardless of the court surface. An opponent should be constantly on her guard against any spin or speed so that she cannot establish a grooved return. All of these serves require placement, depth, and the element of surprise.

Slice Your Serve

On low-bouncing courts such as carpet, Supreme Court, grass, or slow red clay, slice your serve. On carpet surfaces the slice serve grabs well and is very effective. Supreme Court plays much the same way, with perhaps a higher bounce. On the grass courts, slice, slice, slice. The ball will stay extremely low and may even skid. Any opponent will have a rough time hitting a big return if your serve is slicing away from them. On grass you can effectively slice short and wide as well as deeply. As a leftie I like to slice my opponents very wide off the ad court, and on the deuce side I will deliver my serve from a few feet wide of the center line and slice down the "T." A rightie should slice the opposite way—pull your opponent wide on the deuce side and down the middle on the ad. Everyone should slice their second serves.

Kick Your Serve

On slow, high-bouncing courts such as cement or fast clay, kick your serve. On these courts it is pointless really to trash the ball, because the court surface will automatically diminish your power. A kick serve can be very effective here. The higher-bouncing serve is more difficult for your opponent to generate pace from, and she will be forced to reply to a kick from farther back, giving the server more time to come in and the returner more territory to cover. A kick serve should also be used to surprise opponents on the other surfaces—it's a good change-up spin and can give many players trouble. If you've got a lot of confidence in your kick, you should use it as a second serve as well, but do not go to a kick in a very tight situation if you don't feel as though you truly own it. An aborted kick delivery has absolutely no spin to it and is a terrible thing to see, let alone hit. This serve takes confidence as well as know-how.

Hit Them Flat

On fast surfaces hit the ball flat, and even then use this serve sparingly. You always want to be maintaining a high percentage of first serve in, and trying to waste the ball seriously damages your numbers every time. If you happen to own a very large serve, by all means use it, but use it wisely. If you are up in a game by a few points—say, 30–0 or 40–15—let it fly. If I find myself up by a very comfortable margin I may really go for an outrageous launch, giving the nod to speed over percentage, but I've got to feel very cozy to do it. I just don't like the odds on flat serves enough to give them a lot of air time. In serving, as in the rest of tennis, the percentages win for you, not the muscle.

Getting a high percentage of first serves in is as important to the baseliner as it is to the serve-and-volley player. A baseliner may not want to follow her serve into the net, but she also does not want her opponent to attack and come in. Keep missing those first serves and you will surely become defensive about it. The serve is the only stroke that a player is in total control of. That kind of advantage should not be squandered. Whatever type of player you are, use your serve to the fullest.

The Second Serve

There's an old saying, "You're only as good as your second serve." I've got the feeling that a lot of you have blanched upon reading this news. The fact is, most players' glaring weakness is their second delivery, and this is as true in the top ranks as it is at the club level. Do not let your second serve cost you. It should be practiced constantly, because the better your second serve is, the more confidence you will have on your first.

The motion on the second serve is no different than on the first except that you want to impart far more spin on the ball to ensure a safe ride. Do not slow down or abbreviate your motion on the second serve—if anything, you should speed up the motion from the backswing on through so that you will get more work on the ball. Generally players do just the opposite and lose any possible spin.

Except for myself, Pam Shriver, and Barbara Potter, there are few players who follow their second serves to net. For this reason it is not that important to make a pinpoint placement on the second serve. Think of getting the ball high over the net and deep into the service box, preferably to the weaker side. In doubles you should come to the net behind both serves. Make certain that you get to the net as quickly as possible off your second serve because your opponent will be taking a bigger whack at it than she would on your first. If the serve is too bad to come in behind, stay back on it, but always look for the first opportunity to join your partner at the net.

Serving Drills

The best way to practice serving is to use targets— either buckets, or pyramids made of tennis balls—and station them at various angles within the serving box. Aim for the targets and make sure that you do not just work on your favorite serve but on all of the serves—

flat, slice, kick, and wide, deep, and shallow. You can practice hitting twenty down the middle, twenty to the corners, and twenty second serves. Practice against another player so that you can gauge each serve's effectiveness.

Serving practice can seem boring at times, but the extra work you do—a bucket of balls a day—will give your serve consistency, rhythm, and added power. And by keeping the drills interesting you will enjoy yourself and take even more advantage of this vitally important and too-often underdeveloped part of the game.

The Return of Serve

There are many players who fail to realize that the return of serve is a stroke all its own and that neglecting this very important aspect of the game is probably costing them a lot of points. These players generally tend to treat the return like any other groundstroke, when in fact the return of serve is a much closer relative to the volley. The proper stance is similar to that of the volley, the backswing is greatly abbreviated, and the wrist is firm and sure. On most serves the return is more of a block than a full-bodied swing, with the racket head a bit lower than on a volley.

You should start out returning serve from about two to three feet behind the baseline, and sometimes even closer, depending on the power of the server. If your opponent's serves fall shorter than that, move in. Also move in if her serve is very flat. By taking the ball early with a slice return you have countered some of her punch. If your opponent moves you wide with her serves, shade over a bit toward the alleys. And, of course, always move in a bit behind second serves.

A good return of serve requires reflexes and agility. You can often take your cue on direction and pace of the oncoming serve from your opponent's service toss. As you read her toss, turn your shoulders. Your racket, which is held out in front of you at the start of the toss, will then automatically pivot with your shoulder. Your weight should be forward, on the balls of your feet, and your feet should be comfortably apart. You should be in a slightly crouched but basically upright position—any lower and you will not be able to move laterally with any kind of ease. Now take your backswing, and remember to keep it short—if properly executed, you needn't supply any additional power by winding up to the ball. If you want to haul off on a serve, step back a bit and take a fuller swing. Make contact in front of your body, and keep your follow-through long and smooth. And always be moving forward as you hit the ball.

Do not forget to practice your returns as much as possible. Any time someone wants to practice her serve, ask if you can practice returning.

The Half Volley

The half volley is a shot that combines a groundstroke and a volley, a pickup shot hit immediately after the ball bounces at midcourt. Because the ball is so low, the stroke is considered a defensive one, but that is not necessarily the case if you are quick and agile and wish to take your opponent by surprise. As a matter of

24A   24B

Fig. 24 *The half volley*

fact, I play a lot of my winning drop shots off half
volleys because it is a nice place to use my touch and
I do not have to generate or oppose any kind of power
from the half-volley position.

To prepare for a half volley your eyes must be trained
on the ball, and your racket must be in position. The
racket should be slightly open-faced and there is little
if any backswing involved. Stay down. The natural
tendency is to jump off the half volley early, before
the follow-through is over, but this will cause the ball
to sit up and beg to be punished. Get down almost to
your knees—I have scraped mine plenty of times while
executing half volleys. Make contact slightly in front
of your body, and finish the shot as you would a

24C

24D

24E

groundstroke, with a long, smooth follow-through. Go for depth on this shot, and for the most part send your half volleys cross-court so that you can take advantage of the drop in net height. Once you have hit your half, advance into the volley position; don't scurry back to the baseline. Hit your shot and don't look back.

The Approach Shot

An approach shot is supposed to get you comfortably into the net area. The approach sets up the point at net, it does not win it. The best approaches are those that are hit deeply into your opponent's court, those that either get your opponent on the run (in the corners) or deny your opponent any angles to hit off of (right down the middle), or, if you are playing on grass or other slick courts, those that barely clear the net, forcing your opponent to play up on the ball or miss completely. The approach shot must be aggressive. It cannot be hit high over the net, softly, or midcourt. A lot of people who shy away from the net do so because they constantly are getting passed. It is likely that these people do not spend enough time working on their approach shot, the shot needed to set up their volley. My thinking is the better I can make my approach shot, the easier a time I will have at net.

The approach shot looks like an overextended volley. The racket head is up high with a slightly open face, the shoulders are turned sideways to the net, and the wrist is locked solid. The backswing is minimal. You want to be using the pace generated from your opponent's shot and transferring your body weight forward

into the ball. It is very important to take the ball well
out in front of your body. You will be moving forward
as you hit, so there is a tendency to see yourself at net
before you even make contact with the ball. Do not
overrun the shot. Keep your elbows tucked in close to
your body and make the swing short and sweet and
firm as possible.

More often than not I will slice like this on both my
forehand and backhand approaches. This makes the ball
come into my opponent's court low and hard and with
a nice little bite to it. I've got a sidespin approach on
my forehand down the line that I sometimes use to pull
my opponent even farther off the court, and I sometimes use a flat approach shot as well, but that is only
when the ball is high and I can use my approach more
or less as an outright winner. I also get off a topspin
forehand approach shot every now and then, but this is
a difficult shot and I need a slow-moving short ball to
hit. A down-the-line slice is my most basic and safest approach to the net. The slice gives me control and is the
easiest spin to produce on the run, and hitting down
the line is the quickest way to the net and allows me
to cover the angles best. A cross-court approach leaves
my down-the-line side wide open, so the only appropriate time for a cross approach is when I've got my
opponent on the run and off the court. But whether
or not I approach down the line or cross-court, I always
aim about three or four feet inside the sideline. Missing
your approach wide is a sin, since you are not even
giving your opponent a shot at missing. Save yourself
this aggravation by keeping your shots a few feet within
the boundaries.

Percentage-wise, when approaching down the line,

you will most likely get a cross-court shot back, so move over slightly. When approaching cross-court, you need to cover the down-the-line shot since that part of the court will be wide open.

Approach-Shot Drills

Billie Jean King made up an approach-shot drill, and it's not easy. Before the drill begins, Billie Jean will stipulate to her partner that she must take a certain number ball—the third of the rally, or the fourth—and use it for an approach shot, regardless of where it lands. This gets really tough sometimes, but the intent of the drill is a good one because it forces you to make a deliberate approach and it stresses depth on the ball.

This drill can involve either two players against one, or one against one. Everyone starts at the baseline, trading groundstrokes until one of the players hits short. The other uses this to come in behind and must play out the point. Play to 11 points and see who wins the game and from what part of the court—the baseline or the net.

The Overhead

The motion on the overhead is very similar to that of the serve because the ball is met above the body and driven out and downward into the court. As in the serve, you must be standing behind the ball, and you must extend your body for as long as possible. Many people get overly anxious to see where their smash is heading, and they forget to finish their swing. A long follow-through is necessary to a good overhead, so put a healthy finish on your stroke before you come off it to see where you've hit.

The overhead demands both power and control, and the timing necessary for a solid smash means that you must practice this stroke constantly. I had neglected my own overhead for a long time, and to this day I still don't get enough depth on my smashes. But I work a lot harder on it now, and my angles and putaways win me points in every match.

Once you recognize that a lob is being launched, get your racket up any way you can. Unlike in the serve, you are not in control of the ball's flight. Your opponent dictates that, so your backswing cannot be an elaborately timed affair. I just get my racket straight up and over my head—no fancy deal at all. As a leftie my right arm is extended outward toward the oncoming ball for balance and alignment. My shoulder is turned the same way as for a serve. The big mistake made by most players is trying to make contact while squarely facing the net. Turn so that you generate plenty of body power into the shot and keep the shoulders turned for as long as possible. Remember also to keep your head up and watch the ball intently. By keeping your head up, your entire body—your shoulders, arms, everything—will be better balanced and aligned, like a dancer's.

The actual "hit" should be sharp and powerful and produced with an air of finality. If you want to smash the ball flat, get directly under it. If you wish to give the ball less speed and more spin, make contact slightly more in front of your body. If the ball has gotten over your head, you will have to leap at the ball. In this

25A

25B

Fig. 25 *The forehand overhead*

25E

25E

25F

25F

25C

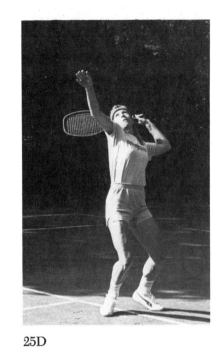

25D

25G

25H

case you will need to add some spin and go for angles, not power.

When you've made up your mind what you are going to do with the smash, forget about your opponent and just watch the ball. Even if she has guessed your intentions, keep your original pick for the shot, or you will doubtless flub the overhead. Do not be afraid to hit two or three smashes before you win the point. You want to be "safely aggressive." Don't ever hit your overheads too softly or too close to the lines, and practice smashing as you would practice any other stroke in this book. This will beef up your net game and instill confidence in you while discouraging a lob-inclined opponent from a favorite strategy.

The Backhand Overhead

A small opponent is going to play her lobs to your backhand side. You will be swinging with a lot less power from there, so the best shot to play off her lob is an acute angle cross-court. You make contact with the ball above your head, just as for the regular smash, but the stroke is very short and compact and as aggressive as possible. You will not be able to generate any real wrist snap, so your best play is for a wide and short cross-court shot that will pull your opponent off into the seats.

Overhead Drill

When practicing my overhead I warm it up slowly. My practice partner will feed me overheads while standing in the middle of the baseline. I will hit the

26A

26B

Fig. 26 *The backhand overhead*

26C

first few smashes directly back to my partner, then angle into the corners. I practice hitting into every corner of the court, some with lots of depth, some sharply angled and shallow. Proper direction is easy for me to achieve, but I must work hard on power and control. For that I use this overhead drill.

I play the net, and my partner is on the baseline, hitting lobs. I must aim my smashes back to my partner. If they are too far from her, we replay the point. I can win a point only by bouncing my smash over my practice partner's head, by forcing her to miss her reply lob, or by hitting right through her. This could get very tiring because sometimes it can take as many as twenty overheads before either player misses. But generally the net player should win the game. Play to 11 points, or only 7 if you get too tired and work your way up to 11.

The Drop Shot

Like the lob, the drop shot is best used sparingly. It is good to hit a drop shot when you could be playing the same ball another way. The drop comes in handy when you are trying to tire your opponent, when you want to surprise her with a change of pace, or when you want to drag her into the net and then drive or lob past her. The shot requires good hands and a delicate touch and should not be performed when you are off-balance or on the run. It is a shot that I use now more than ever before in my matches, and, directly or indirectly, I win a lot of points with this deft little move.

The start of your drop shot should not look different from the start of your forehand or backhand slice. But you hold your racket a little bit looser and quit on the stroke right before you make contact with the ball. Though you must hold up and slow down your motion, you still put a slight finish on the stroke—you almost caress the ball, strum it off your strings. On my backhand drop shot I use my wrist to scoop the ball over the net. On my forehand drop shot, I actually recoil off my stroke. As I make contact I pull my racket off the ball. I do the same thing on my drop volleys. I open up my racket face and recoil at the point of impact. I feel like I am setting a baby down in a bed of pillows, almost. There is a lot of softness required here.

If you wish to use the drop shot in your game, remember to try it only when you are in front of the baseline, and then only if the score suggests the opportunity. If you try the drop from beyond the baseline your opponent will see it coming and belly up to the net immediately. And because the drop shot and drop volley are such delicate pieces of work, you must play to the score to use them wisely. It can be difficult to feather a shot just barely over the net when the pressure is on, the wind is up, and your opponent moves like a deer. Use your knowledge of percentages and a lot of sound judgment when you go for the touch shots. (See p. 116.)

Drills for Touch Shots

During any kind of drilling that you are involved in, go for the soft stuff every now and then. Use the drop shot and drop volley as once-in-a-while options, and be sure that they are disguised to look like your normal strokes. You can practice going from a drive to a slice

27A

27B

Fig. 27 *The backhand dropshot*

27D

27E

27C

to a drop. Place a bucket just over the net on your practice partner's side, and every now and then she should call out, "drop shot" to you. See how close to the moment of contact your partner can wait before you effectively make the drop, and count how many times you find the bucket, or at least come close. Practice your drop volley the same way, by placing a target on the court and by mixing in a short volley with the regular volleys you hit in your drills.

The Lob

I am going to use this space to lobby for better lobbing. The lob is one of the most misunderstood strokes in the game. So few players understand just how effective good lobbing can be, both defensively and offensively. On defense, a lob can keep you alive in a point if you are out of position and require some recovery time. It's a perfect tool for when your opponent is at the net and you do not have a good play on a passing shot. It can dislodge a mighty and relentless serve-and-volley opponent from the net, and if your opponent is dictating the rally, a thoughtful lob can change the pace and break up your opponent's commanding rhythm. Offensively, a well-disguised lob can be an outright winner. It can force your opponent to play farther from the net than she likes, denying her all of the short-court angles. An offensive lob will also allow you time to get to the net yourself.

A lob should look very similar to a regular groundstroke so that your opponent cannot guess your intention and back up, ready for the kill. The lob requires a shorter backswing, an open racket face, and an upward motion. The follow-through on a lob is slightly abbreviated but smooth. Do not end the stroke too abruptly or your lob will fall short of its mark. Proper height and depth are the keys. On defensive lobs, send the ball very high and close to the baseline area. Most players hit their lobs too short, so remember that it's better to lob too long than too short. A short ball will give your opponent a tasty meal at the net. A ball hit long always stands the chance of being miscalculated and played by your opponent anyway. A good offensive lob, whether topspinned or sliced, should barely escape the racket of your opponent. That way she will have no chance to run down the lob and make a return off your shot. Topspin lobs are very difficult to produce, and you should go for one only if your opponent is really blanketing the net and you mean to discourage her.

I use the lob more often in doubles than singles, as a return of serve, to gain access to the net, to force the opposite team to play farther back from the net area, and, in general, to break up the rhythm of the rallies. I will employ the lob often under dodgy weather conditions. No one enjoys hitting overheads in the glare of the sun, and not many players rub their hands eagerly when they see a lob being buffeted toward them by gusting winds either. The idea is to give them more than they bargained for. I will also use my lob more on clay and slow, hard courts than on the other surfaces because it is easier to chase down overhead replies on the slower surfaces than on the slick and faster ones. Although I try to avoid lobbing against someone with a truly fine overhead, I will still hoist a couple to her every now and then merely to keep her from playing tight to the net. One final rule: I always lob to my opponent's backhand. The backhand overhead is a much more difficult shot to play because of the limited upper-body strength on that side. Lobbing to the correct side of an oponent's body can mean the difference between giving her exactly what she wants (an overhead smash) or precisely what she dreads (a backhand overhead). The choice, of course, is yours, but I prefer to watch my opponent squirm than squeal with delight. (See p. 120.)

Lobbing Drills

The same drill that is used for the overhead is excellent for the lobber involved, so practice that drill for

28A

28B

Fig. 28 *The backhand lob*

28D

28E

28C

both strokes. Another way to practice your lob is to
have your practice partner position herself at the net
and hit you deep volleys. You must lob her balls high
and deep into the backcourt, aiming into both corners
so that you can play a leftie's backhand as well as a
rightie's. Always practice hitting some lobs on the run.
Instead of going for the big shot all the time, practice
lofting them, too. Constantly work on your disguise,
and lob the ball when the situation could easily call
for a drive or a sliced ball instead. Any magician will
tell you that the art of deception takes a lot of practice.
Deceptive lobbing takes a lot of work.

Passing Shots

I see many players panic when they are forced to hit a passing shot. Their opponent has come to net and suddenly they are wild with anxiety. They rush their normal stroke, hit the ball harder than it deserves to be hit, and forget the thought of finishing with a full swing. Does this sound like you? Well, calm down and relax. The passing shot is like any other groundstroke you hit, only you must play the ball closer to the lines. You certainly do not have to add pace to the ball, unless you're the headhunter type who likes to drill the passing shot right through her opponent. You needn't concern yourself with depth either, because all you want to do is get the ball by your net-playing opponent. As long as the ball lands in the court, you have won the point. So the most important ingredient in a passing shot is direction. Placement and a little bit of poise will give you a good, solid weapon against any net rusher.

If your opponent is tall, hit your passes cross-court. The ball will be low and at her feet, making for a very demanding volley. If your opponent is short or lacks quickness, send your shot down the line. Her limited reach and speed will not allow her to cover that far across the net.

If you are made to hit a passing shot off a deep ball, send it down the line. It is more difficult to intercept than a cross-court reply. If the ball is very deep, then your best play is to lob, unless you can muscle the ball past your opponent, Ivan Lendl style. If the approach shot is within the baseline area, go cross-court. That's where the percentages are.

Passing-Shot Drills

A two-on-one drill, with two people at the baseline against one at the net, playing to 11 points, is a good drill, and you can reverse it so that there is one at the baseline and two at the net. No lobs are allowed—you must try to hit by or through the player to win. Targets set up on different areas of the court can improve your passing shots. Have your partner try to defend the targets against your attack, then switch. A great passing-shot drill is called "King of the Net" and is best played when you've got at least four players. One player takes the net and another player or coach is the feeder of balls. The feeder will hit five balls to the remaining players, one at a time, and the first player to win 3 out of 5 points against the net player "dethrones" that player and is crowned the new king. Lobs are allowed, but not off the fed ball. The player who reigns the longest wins.

Hitting on the Run

When you are forced to hit the ball on the run it means that your opponent has gotten control of the point. It does not necessarily mean that you will lose the rally, but you will be hard pressed to win it. You should either lob the ball very high and deeply, as Tracy Austin does so well, or you should go for a winner. A lob will keep you in the point and give you a chance to recover some court. Hit high enough, the lob can suddenly put your opponent on the defensive, because timing a very high lob is tricky. If you decide you want to go for the gusto, hit the ball down the line. A down-the-liner is a lot easier to produce on the run than a cross-courter because you do not have to finish the stroke all the way across your body. What you must always do while on the run is remember to get height on your ball. The net is six inches higher near the posts than it is in the middle, so a down-the-line shot has to be higher than a cross-court shot. Too many players miss their running shots into the net, which is a very depressing way to lose the point. As you bolt to the ball, concentrate on clearing the net at all costs. Then weigh your possibilities and go for it. There is no use choking on your running shot because you have been outmaneuvered so that you have lost the battle of percentages. Have a good old time with it—this is usually where the "hero" shots are made, the real crowd-pleasers.

A lot of people watch me play but get disgruntled when they see me agonize over a difficult running shot that I have missed. What they do not realize is that I am not expressing anger over the last shot I played, but over the series of shots I hit leading up to the miss that put me in that terrible position of weakness. I am not suggesting that you look aggravated, as I sometimes do, when you miss a shot on the run. What I am suggesting is that you think back on how you got yourself into such a precarious position and correct the error so you do not make the same mistake over and over again and blame the loss of the point on your last shot. Back up the film and you will find where the true loss of the point actually originated. This could save your sneakers and a lot of wear and tear.

Where to Stand at the Net

To play the net aggressively you must be close enough to take advantage of all of the potentially winning angles without making yourself susceptible to your opponent's lob. The ideal place to volley from is about six feet from the net. Any farther back and you will be volleying up on the ball, and any closer to the net will deny you a forward thrust into the ball and means that you can move only sideways to cover a passing shot. It is a lot easier to move forward than backward, and you will have that much more time to read your opponent's pass.

When playing the net in doubles, you must give the impression that you may poach at any time, even though it may be seldom that you cross and cut off a shot. The general tendency is to guard the alley too much, which gives your opponents an awful lot of court to hit into. Take an aggressive posture when playing net in doubles by shading off the alley lines by a few feet. If your opponents keep scorching you by threading down your alley, of course you should blanket it more completely. But by positioning yourself more toward the center of the court you force the other team to make better returns and sharper angles, and there is a good chance that your presence will force errors and overhit shots. If you decide that you are going to poach a ball, make it very decisive and go for a winner. Poaches are forever.

Playing Tactics and Strategies

I like to think of myself as an all-court player, although I do try to come into the net as often as I can. The type of player you are depends upon what kind of athlete you are, what abilities and skills you possess, and what your mental attitude toward the game is like.

I was always naturally drawn to the net, where it was challenging to hit quick volleys, have good reflexes, and finish the point as soon as possible. I hated the idea of waiting around on the baseline for my opponent to make a mistake, or to rally with her endlessly, patiently tiring her out of the match. I just never had the temperament for that kind of play. Of course, there are challenges to this style, but they are not the challenges I would choose to meet.

An all-around player should not have any weaknesses. A solid all-court player is comfortable at the net but does not necessarily look for every chance to take the hill at all cost—she can stay on the baseline as well. Evonne Goolagong Cawley is a good example of an all-court player. Rosie Casals and Wendy Turnbull use the entire court well, too. Because of their sizes, perhaps, Rosie and Wendy do not play every shot to get to the net. They would require more height and reach for such a relentless attack. But from wherever they play on the court they are the aggressors, and that is what makes them win. It also explains how the shortest doubles team in the game is also one of the winningest.

A player like Pam Shriver is the typical serve-and-volley player, one who comes in on every ball, rain or shine, sometimes at the wrong moment. This is exactly what I used to do to excess. I would charge in behind everything. I would hit a ball that would only reach my opponent's service line, but in I'd storm, hoping that she would feel threatened by the boldness of my move and miss her passing shot, or reply weakly enough for me to get off a winning volley. This, of course, is a risky way to go about winning tennis matches, and when you've hit the big time it just does not get the job done. It takes fine seasoning and refinement to cultivate an attacking brand of tennis.

I love serve-and-volley tennis because it feels great when you are dictating the tempo of the match, forcing the plays, and the baseline opponent can only answer what you do, merely react to your shots. I can force my opponent to pick up her own pace and deliver returns she is not comfortable with. In effect I can bully her around the court. There is a saying that you are only as good as your opponent, but I like to think that my opponent is only as good as I allow her to be. Obviously not everyone can think this way, but it is a good attitude to take to the court with you. Try to force your opponent into playing your game, and whatever you do, don't play hers. Do not be lured into her style of tennis, answering to her tactics and pace and falling prey to her pet shots. Do what you know best and stick with it. Stay with your strengths and cover up your weaknesses as best you can.

"Always change a losing game and never change a winning game." How many times have you heard that one? But it is so true. At all times be aware of the flow of the match, and be mindful of what is winning you points and costing you points. You have to walk out on the court with some plan in mind, some predetermined perceptions and judgments of both yourself and your opponent. If your method of attack is backfiring on you, slow down and decide why. Are you coming in behind a weak approach? Is your opponent feeding off the pace you are giving her? Are you trying to end the points too abruptly? Determine whether you are using the wrong tactics or whether you are just executing the proper tactics badly, and then make your adjustments. Do not get jumpy and begin to press too much when you feel as though your game has stepped out for lunch. Players tend to overhit the ball when they are behind, and they end up hustling themselves right out of their own matches. If this happens to you, relax. Pull your thoughts together and believe that there's just got to be some way to win. Change the pace around. Keep your opponent guessing as to what is coming off of your strings next. If she is erratic, make her play long, complicated points. If she avoids the net, call her up with some drop shots. Toss up some lobs, sting some forehands. And be sure to look as unruffled as possible. It's not always easy, and I don't always do it, but it is a great edge if you can keep your emotions close to your necktie.

Serve and Volley

I think the serve-and-volley player has to be more aware of the score than the baseline player does. I say this as a server-and-volleyer, because I know that I just cannot come in on any and every shot. The idea of picking my spots with great care is something that Renee Richards has helped me with immeasurably.

Knowing when to serve and volley is particularly important on clay courts, where you must construct a truly aggressive stance before you attack. Clay surfaces are going to take the sting out of your shots. The ball grabs the surface and is slowed down considerably, allowing much more reaction time for your opponent. I have seen a lot of big-serving, hard-hitting pros look downright silly trying to figure out what to do on clay, while their much smaller South American opponents are taking their best stuff and strumming it back to them, eager for more. I am not saying that you should completely abandon your style to slow surfaces, but you must make concessions to them.

When you attack, make sure to do so off a good serve or a short ball. If you are given a ball around the service line or shorter, come in behind it. Do not try to take the hill when you are standing five or six feet behind the baseline. From that position you cannot get close enough to the net for a decent volley, and your opponent will then be replying from an offensive, not a defensive, position.

As you come into the net area, remember to run your opponent from side to side with your shots. Your approach does not have to be extremely deep or solid if your opponent is being forced to run. Everyone is less effective on the run. Having to chase a ball cuts down on accuracy, depth, and pace, so your chances of winning a point against a dancing opponent are good. Keep in mind, however, that the more you drag your opponent around the court, the more conceivable angles you create for her. Be prepared to reply to sharply placed passing shots or lobs. Your opponent may get some by you, but tennis is a game of percentages. The more you force the issue with sound serves and volleys, the greater the chances that the scales will tip in your favor. Constantly asking your opponent to come up with ambitious angles and lobs is a great way to frustrate her and draw errors.

I would not recommend serving and volleying off a second serve, no matter how good a second serve you've got. There are some players, like Shriver, who own truly great second serves—high-kicking affairs that give her opponents all kinds of headaches. But the fact remains that once you have missed your first serve your opponent invariably says to herself, "Okay, now I'll have a really good chance to have a crack at the ball." Such opponents will think that they are on top of you, and it will be reflected in their play. They will adopt a positive attitude about the point and play it with a psychological and emotional edge. The only times I could see where it could be a good idea is if you are going for a surprise move, or if you are sitting on top of a 40–0 lead and feel very comfortable.

When I am serving at 30–40 I usually stay back on the baseline after my serve and avoid the chancy stuff. You must always try to hold onto your service game, of course, and I tend to play a little bit safer when I am staring at a break point. If I am given the oppor-

tunity to force the action, I will by all means, despite
the score. For instance, if I get off a really good serve
on a break point I will follow in on it although I had
not planned to, because I can expect a high return
for an easy volley.

In playing against a serve-and-volley player, it becomes very important to return the serve well. If the
server sends you off the court wide, your best play is to
return down her line. If you are getting served down
the middle of the court, return the serve down the middle and low—to her shoetops, if possible. Of course,
you must mix up your returns, standing in on some
to take them early, standing back on others to allow
more time for a full-bodied crack at the ball. The lob
will keep the server from climbing on top of the net,
and short cross-court returns are effective to break up
the routine and force the server to lose some ground.
Practice your passing shots as well as your returns, and
be sure to keep a good length on all of your groundstrokes. You just know that a serve-and-volley player is
waiting for a short one.

Baseline Tactics

I have learned a lot about baseline tennis from playing
on clay, and with the years I have grown comfortable
with my groundstrokes. Good baseliners, like good
servers-and-volleyers, understand how to open up the
court and draw the short ball from their opponents.
My personal feeling is that serve-and-volley tennis
players have to be more exacting and more precise than
baseline tennis players and that they require better
timing and reflexes. Baseliners learn how to play their

games quicker than servers-and-volleyers, and for this reason baseliners mature much earlier. The ground-stroke is the bread-and-butter stroke of tennis, and the fact that more points are lost than won explains the successes of Christ Evert Lloyd and Tracy Austin. Their groundstrokes are so solid and consistent that they hardly ever make any unforced errors. They play the highest percentage shots possible, but both these play-ers also hit with great accuracy and power, enabling them to hit winners from the baseline. This would be tough to do for little kids, or even for big kids like me. But more important than pace is depth. A good base-line player keeps the ball deep and moves it all around the court in a very consistent fashion, anticipating a weak response. Having opened up the court, she will then look to finish the point in much the same way a server-and-volleyer would. Clearly there are champions of both styles, and the most interesting matches usually involve contrasting game plans.

If you play a baseline game and your opponent is not error-prone and also happens to have a decent net game, then the advantage is with her. For this reason, do not neglect your short-court game. You should be comfortable enough to chase down a drop shot or spoon up a half volley and not be petrified at the thought of it. Any clear-thinking opponent knows enough to coax a confirmed baseliner to the net.

In general, what I would recommend is that you treat all of your strokes equally. A serve-and-volley player still needs sound groundies and should not con-centrate solely on her forward game. A baseliner should not leave only the final five minutes of her practice ses-sions to take a few at the net. Do not overlook your weaknesses, but be sure not to overwork them at the expense of losing your strengths. If your forehand wins you matches, be sure you keep it singing. Pay attention to your backhand side, but never drop your guns, your most precious weapons.

How to Play the Big Points

If I am ahead at the time of a big point I will go for it a lot more than if I am down. It is a rare scene when a top pro does not become slightly more conservative on the biggies, and I am no exception. I will not squander a lead by making foolish mistakes, going for the hero shots. I always try to play the percentages on the big points. I used to go for the cute shots, but no more. I have learned to use my strengths to the maximum in the pivotal points of a match, and you must learn to do this, too. If your best shot is a forehand cross-court pass and you are given that shot to play, by all means play that shot. Do not try to surprise your opponent by sliding one down the line. Sometimes this is a glorious idea and the plan to cross up your opponent will work, but remember what your best percentages are and stick with the numbers. If you are placed in a position where you can be aggressive and make something happen, then go for it.

When things are getting more and more intense, do not try to go for the lines unless you are absolutely forced to thread the needle by your opponent. This would happen more often in doubles than in singles. In either case, always give yourself as much margin for error as you can. There is no reason to hit the ball wide or in the net on a big point. Missing long is okay because it shows that you are still stroking the ball and giving it a good ride, and there is always the chance that your opponent will try to hit a ball that is sailing long. Hitting in the net or wide of the sidelines does not even give your opponent the chance to miss. Your shots should be aimed two or three feet inside of the sideline and a few safe feet over the net. If you are a net rusher, you especially should not squander the approaches. You do not win points on approach shots, so you should not lose points there either. Hit your approaches deep. Run your opponent all over the court and make her win the point by passing you. Dare her to come up with the big shot at the right time. It won't be easy.

When I get tight under pressure my strokes become shorter, more rigid, and my shots become far less penetrating. What I try to do is hit out on the ball more. I try to relax. It is not easy trying to tell yourself to relax if you happen to be serving at 4–5 in the third set and you are down a break point, but it helps if you slow down for a fraction of a moment and tell yourself to breathe deeply. Proper breathing is important in order for the body to function well, particularly under stressful situations. I am continually taking large gulps of air when there is tough sledding ahead. Breathing deeply gives you a fresh supply of oxygen and loosens up your ever-constricting muscles.

You can also move your feet. Footwork tends to break down more than anything else when the pressure is on. Your strokes may be holding up beautifully, but you would never know it because your lower body has become paralyzed with fear. What you think is poor stroke production is actually a staggered arrival to the ball that is making you late to your shots. Make a concerted effort to sight the ball right off the strings of your opponent and bolt to it.

Try hitting out more. Do not hit the ball out of the court, but really take a whack at it. This is just possibly the last thing in the world that you honestly feel like doing when the time comes, but it is actually a great way to relax and regain your diminishing stroke. You can only proceed with confidence on this if you put a lot of topspin on your shots. The more work you put on the ball, the safer a shot you produce, which should be a very comforting thought. Also, by swinging away like this the pressure of the moment subsides because your shots are becoming safer as your opponent is getting tagged with more pace and spin to reply to. She will undoubtedly think that you have the heart and courage of ten players. And remember, you do not have to be strong to hit topspin, merely technically sound.

Concentrate on each shot. There should be no loose points here. You cannot afford to give away freebies on the big points. This should come easy to you, as you should not have to tell yourself to concentrate when the score is 6-all. Do not let your opponent toss off your concentration by lulling you into a sense of complacency and making you feel safe. That is when an opponent can really burn you with some forceful or surprising shots.

You should observe Barbara Potter, the leftie from Connecticut, when she is playing a tie breaker. Pottsy has a very impressive tie-breaker winning record for several reasons. She knows how to keep her cool under the gun, and she owns a punishing first serve, which is a lovely thing to have handy when trying to decide a set. Apart from maintaining your composure and serving well, you should again remember to play the percentages for all they're worth. No cute stuff when the scoreboard says it's tied at 6. I have learned the hard way that this is not the time to endear yourself to the fans. In a tie breaker you are not playing for the crowd; you are playing for yourself.

How to Use Your Strengths

You should be more aware than anyone of what your strengths and weaknesses are, mentally as well as physically. You must completely understand your own game and your own emotions. If you know that you get uptight on your opponent's serve, deal with it, whether that means jumping up and down a bit to loosen up, hitting out on the return more, or changing the pace of your replies. If, on the other hand, your return of serve is your greatest asset, know that too and make the most of it.

Stick with what you win with. John Newcombe and Jaroslav Drobny had similar games—big serves, big forehands, and minor backhands. Though their games were incomplete, they knew just how to win with what they owned. Virginia Ruzici of Romania is the same way. Huge forehand, mediocre backhand. She can be very tough. When I play Ruzici, I can be sure that if I am serving at 30–40 she will be looking to run around her backhand on either serve and go for broke off her forehand. Sue Barker, Great Britain's former number one, will do the same thing. They'll go for the gusto, especially when it counts the most.

Exploiting Your Opponent's Weaknesses

The best way to shut down your opponent is to pick on weak spots, but you cannot constantly play to deficiencies. If my opponent has a weak or limited backhand side, I will naturally play to it a lot, but if I were to keep my shots there for too long she could either get a good groove going and become comfortable from there, or she could anticipate my tactic and be ready for a backhand so far in advance that she'd be able to run around it and block a forehand. To get to your opponents' weaknesses you must sometimes play to their strengths, no matter what they've got to hurt you with. Even if I had to play Ivan Lendl, whose forehand is scary, I would not try to avoid it all day long—he would then know exactly what was coming off my strings. Besides, he could get overanxious with his forehand and make some unforced errors, and when the confidence in your best stroke erodes, it is extremely difficult to play aggressively. Keep your opponents moving and guessing all the time.

With most people it is easy to spot their weakness, whether it be their serve, their overhead, or their backhand. Other players' weaknesses are not as visible, and then you must carefully seek out what they do not enjoy hitting. It could be that your opponent is uncomfortable with low volleys, or perhaps she misses a lot of high volleys. She may have a rough time hitting balls on the run, or perhaps she is a deft mover from side to side but awkward when running back and forth. If possible, scout your opponent before a match.

Otherwise, once on the court give her a little bit of everything and see how she handles all the situations. Be sure to experiment as the match progresses because weaknesses can surface after the match has begun and your opponent is less relaxed and confident.

Playing Against Little Pace

Often a player has a tougher time handling someone with little pace on their ball than someone who pounds away at it. There are traps that you can fall into very easily. You may start to overswing, thereby overhitting the ball and making frustrating errors. You may become lulled by the slowness of your opponent's ball and lose your own rhythm, so that instead of having plenty of time, you are late on everything. You may just get frustrated by the boring speed of the ball and totally lose your concentration and cool. This could be a very crafty opponent who knows that this tactic will make you squirm. Do not let it happen.

Against such an opponent you must exercise patience and common sense—patience because you will have to hold back at times and attack at others, and you must not hurry by your choices; common sense because this kind of opponent has no real weapon and she forces you to beat yourself. That means you are in more control than you think. Keep your wits about you and treat this player as though she were as dangerous as a serving-and-volleying fool.

From a technical standpoint you will have to make more of a swing in order to generate pace. Your opponent has denied you the kind of pace that you are used to responding to, so be certain not to muscle the ball out of the lines. Prepare far in advance for the ball—do not stroll up to it just because it has taken a while to reach you. That sense of having plenty of time is a false one, and it should not affect or in any way alter the preparation you would give to your strokes. It's always better to get to the ball too early rather than too late. Put plenty of finish on your shots, and avoid the tendency to pull up early to check where the ball has gone. Move quickly, not lackadaisically, to the ball so that you can take it early and force a swifter, hurried reply.

Tactically you must try to break up your opponent's rhythm and choke her plan to make you miss. As soon as you get a ball that you can volley, storm in and put it away. If the slowballer is hitting high and deep, surprise her by coming in around midcourt and play the midcourt volley. If you serve and volley, come in quickly and smother the net—do not get forced into playing off a low chip return. Practice your overheads plenty before the match, because chances are you'll be staring skyward quite a bit out there. If the lobs are very high and you begin to miss, or if they are too hard to judge, bounce them before you play them. Do not overplay the return of serve. A common tendency is for a player to see a light serve float over the court and envision ramming it down her opponent's throat. Do not drool over these serves—you may want to step in and give a couple of them a good ride, but be sure that you don't throw away easy return possibilities by launching returns into neighboring villages. Play the returns back deeply, or angle them sharply off the court. Remember —you will not defeat yourself.

Playing Against a Lot of Pace

Any time you step out on the court you want to be the player controlling the tempo of the match. To be forced to abandon your own pace and speed limit is discomforting and often debilitating. A hard hitter has the power to do this to you. Ivan Lendl spent much of 1982 doing that very thing to John McEnroe, and it took a long time before John figured out how to win against Ivan. Ultimately John returned to his strengths, his serve and volley, and he fought fire with fire. John got tired of swinging off his back foot all the time. He got quicker, smarter, and more alert because Lendl had forced him to, and maybe now the psyche-out factor is gone for good.

Power hitters have the ability to psyche out anybody. When I am playing a heavy hitter, I have to make a conscious effort not to watch her stroking the ball. When I play against Barbara Potter, for instance, I barely look over at her, because the movements that she makes, the windup on her big serve, the whole thing sways me way off my mark. Besides, it is extra important to be aware of the ball off the opponent's strings. By being more alert and watching the ball come off the racket, I get a better idea of the pace produced and the direction of the ball. I also become more aware of the ball's sound upon being struck. The sound can tip you off to just how hard it was nailed.

Use the pace you are being given. On a return of serve, block the ball back. The ball will be traveling so quickly that you do not have to add any extra heat. Every now and then you may want to play a return from far beyond the baseline so that the ball will lose some of its sting by the time you hit it. Then, by all means, swing away. But if you play the rest of the match from back there, you will lose, because you are giving away too much territory in an effort to get a good swipe at the ball. Do not make these sort of concessions. Stand where you normally play from. You will either have to cut your backswing or speed up the entire stroking motion. I suggest that you abbreviate your swing. Do not get into a slugfest with this player. If anything, mix up your shots. Toss up lobs to break up the day, dinks she can't tee off on, and cling to your own strengths. The additional pace on her balls may cause your racket to turn in your hand, so grip a little tighter, especially to volley. A power hitter likes quick points that require little strategy, so the quicker you can adjust to her speed and the longer you can keep her out there, the greater your chances of victory. Power tennis is physically exhausting, so stay in there and hold your ground. Bigger is not always better.

Court Positioning

When I am playing the baseline I stand anywhere from two to four feet behind the line. If I stand any farther back I lose the chance of doing something with a short ball.

It is rare that both myself and my opponent are hitting from the middle of the court. When that is the case, then the middle of the court is obviously the best place to position oneself. But as soon as a player introduces a shot off the center of the court, positioning changes. Once I move my opponent with my shot, I must position myself to reply to any possible answer that she counters with. For instance, if I hit a ball deep to my opponent's forehand side, I know that her two best shots are either a down-the-liner or a sharp cross-court. My job is to bisect those two angles, which puts me a shade on the cross-court side. Wherever I move my opponent, I must know how to bisect the angles of her two best shots. That will put me in the best possible court position every time.

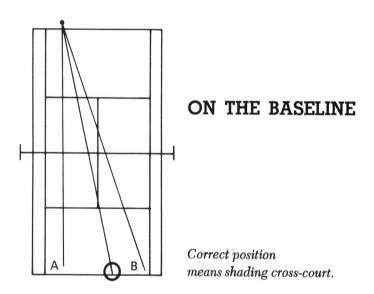

ON THE BASELINE

Correct position means shading cross-court.

Conversely, playing the net means shading to the down-the-line ball on your approach shot. The reason is clear to see in the diagram. The angle of your opponent's ball is cut off much earlier when you are at the net, which means that not all of the possibilities are given a chance to develop. On the same ball as hit in this figure , the net player has cut off the cross-court angle.

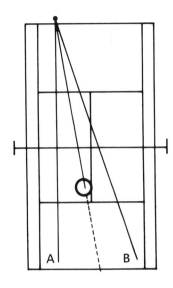

AT THE NET

*Correct position
means shading down the line.*

In other words, the old saying about getting back to the middle of the court after each ball is wrong. Understand the angles of this game and move according to each shot you create. You will find that you are in much more control of the point when you understand how to position yourself on the court. You should practice proper positioning, both at the baseline and at the net, until it becomes automatic to you after every ball. When you know how to defend your territory, the court will seem much smaller to you, much simpler to play on.

How to Play in All Conditions

In the Sunlight

The important thing to remember when playing in sunlight is that for two games you are staring into the sun, but then it's your opponent's turn, so be of good cheer. Do not let the sun bother you too much. It is really only noticeable when you serve or hit overheads. If you are squinting into the sun as you deliver up your toss, you will be forced to alter the toss slightly. You can either move the toss sideways and slice the ball or toss the ball straighter and make contact flatter. The truth is, this is not a problem I am generally faced with because I am a leftie, and normally by the time I play the feature match of the day the sun has gone down quite a bit. But when I play in Australia I have headaches because the sun moves in the opposite direction and the angle of the sunlight is different there. It is then that I remember how to adjust. What is most important is that you have more than one serve, one toss. And if your overhead is having a rotten day, let the ball bounce before you hit it. It is better to take the ball as a regular stroke than to toss your face skyward, close your eyes, and pray that the ball finds the middle of your racket. This maneuver can be highly embarrassing. Bounce the ball and go from there. If the sun is shining in your opponent's eyes, throw that lob up, particularly if you are playing a volleyer. This is a great way to keep her away from the net.

If you are playing under a very hot sun, be certain that your clothes are cool and loose-fitting, that your head is not absorbing too much heat (wear a hat or a visor), and that you towel off not just your face but also your arms and legs. Your body will be much cooler and fresher this way. Be sure to replenish the fluids and salts that your body is losing. Drink a lot of water on changeovers.

In the Wind

Keep it simple when playing on a windy day. If you have big windups on your strokes, try to abbreviate them a bit so that you can adjust more easily to the ball. Do not try to make your shots too good or too precise. You have to play a bit safer. If it's a steady wind that is blowing, you can afford to be a little more ambitious than when you're dealing with a gusty wind or a side wind. With side winds, play to the middle of the court. I have played in such bad side winds that I have actually aimed the ball ten feet from the court, and the wind has blown the ball in for winners, even on a hard hit ball. On a lob the ball can move around a lot more, so in gusty winds, again the play is down the middle. That way you are giving your opponent absolutely no angle, so she may often try to make something out of nothing, overhit the ball, and get totally aggravated. Certainly all approach shots should be aimed down the middle in gusty times.

When you are hitting with the wind, make sure to hit far enough away from the baseline, and put added topspin to your balls. It's a bad idea to try drop shots with the wind—the ball will get blown right to your opponent. You would have to be very precise to pull it off. It is a much better idea to drop-shot when you are against the wind. As a matter of fact, drop shots then are some of your best plays. Be sure that you get good length on your shots when you are against the wind. You can be hitting the ball harder and flatter and aim higher over the net.

As a serve-and-volley player I find it very difficult to be precise and find the middle of the racket in the wind. You can still play the big game, but you must pick your spots very wisely. Even I don't like coming in much under these conditions, but I know that my opponent will be having a hard time hitting precision passing shots, and I use that.

In the Cold

Make certain that you are thoroughly loose and stretched out when playing in the cold or you will pull muscles that you never even knew you owned. Jog around the court for a bit without your racket, then stretch your legs, arms, back, everything. You should wear several layers of clothing that you can peel off as you become acclimated to the temperature.

After you play, stretch again. Then remove any wet articles of clothing and immediately bundle up. Go home. Draw a nice, hot bath for yourself. Lay back and blissfully admire your own courage and fortitude in your battle with the elements.

The Different Court Surfaces

Clay Courts

Clay courts play true, which is one of the reasons I like them. Only the odd divot in a too-soft court or a badly laid line will produce a bad bounce. Another reason I enjoy the clay is because I feel that to win a major clay-court event, such as the French Open, you must play consistently fine tennis, meaning that the best player is rewarded. You can't just get lucky.

The fittest player holds a palpable edge as well, for clay courts demand more stamina than any other surface. You have got to go out on a clay court with the conviction that you will work hard for every single point. Clay will take the bite out of your shots by grabbing onto the ball and slowing it down considerably, so be prepared to hit three or four more shots per rally than you normally would before you are given a ball you can attack. The difficulties in ending a rally quickly will become obvious fast. If you like going for the cheap points, you have gotten off at the wrong surface. Try grass.

Knowing how and when to slide on clay takes a lot of practice and a lot of getting used to. For some players the transition is easy and natural, but for others the surface takes away footing and balance. It should not be such a traumatic adjustment. We are not discussing a lunar surface here, just a soft one. Not all clay courts play the same way. On one clay court you may slide three feet, on others only one foot, depending on how hard the court plays. This can be affected by the amount of rain the court has taken, the texture of the clay, and the thickness of the top dressing. For this reason you must give yourself plenty of time to get to know the court. Just remember that you must always try to get into the best possible court position, because you will be forced to get involved in strategy here more than on any other court.

Sometimes I am guilty of too much sliding, and it

should be avoided as much as possible. You should try to get to the ball without sliding so that you will have better control. Once in a while you will have to slide, but use it only as a last measure.

Keep your balls consistently deep, and move your opponent all over. You must fight for proper position, and you must keep your opponent on the run, up and back, side to side. You must deprive her of preparation time, because a player who is afforded a lot of time to play a ball on clay can carve you up.

The slow surfaces are Billie Jean King's least favorites to play on, but she acknowledges that these surfaces provide her with opportunities denied by the faster courts. She is able to experiment with various spins and slices on clay, stroking and strumming the ball as she can on no other court surface. I share Billie Jean's fascination with spins and slices, and I know that I can be at my artistic best on clay. I do not try to create at the expense of my serve-and-volley game; I merely become a more thoughtful net rusher and expect a lot more shots to come back to me.

Hard Courts

How do I like playing on hard courts? Not a whole lot, to tell you the truth. Hard courts are my least favorite surface, even though I have proven myself on them. The jarring inherent on cement courts is tough on my body, for starters. Also, cement courts can play any number of ways, from very slow, almost clay-like speeds to lightning fast, which favors streaky players and upset artists but not me.

To win consistently on the hard stuff, a player needs

an all-court game because cement will bring out both the server-and-volleyer and the baseliner in you. I find it easier to serve and volley on hard courts than on clay because my serves bounce high and hard, making it possible for me to attack. It is a bit harder for me to come in off rallies because my groundstrokes sit up high enough for my opponents to hit. This makes good approach shots a vital part of my hard-court cool.

One player who really benefits from the properties of the hard court is Pam Shriver. Because of her great height (we tease her when she says she's five-feet-eleven—five-feet-thirteen is closer to the truth), Pam can field the high bounces with ease. To her they are at waist level. It is no fluke that Pam has had such good results at the U.S. Open. She plays her attacking game to the hilt and takes full advantage of her size. Tall people have a distinct advantage on hard courts and should recognize this and reap the advantages.

On hard courts I like to kick my serve a lot and pump loops to my opponent's backhands in anticipation of a high reply. I like to approach the net off a topspin shot for the same reason—by hitting the ball high it becomes difficult for my opponent to hit a low return or a passing shot. Making them bounce high also keeps my opponent pinned to the baseline while allowing me to get closer to the net.

Hard courts will play differently, but good rules to follow are to be a more aggressive baseliner on fast, hard courts and to be a more conservative server-and-volleyer on slow, hard courts. A big serve is a bonus anywhere you play, and hard courts favor a speedy mover, so if you wish to structure an aggressive fore-court attack, you will appreciate hard courts.

Grass Courts

Grass courts are the flukiest of them all. That Bjorn
Borg was able to win five Wimbledon titles in a row is
incredible, but it surely helped Bjorn that the men
play best of five sets instead of best of three. I think
it's tougher for a woman to win Wimbledon. Although
the Big W's courts are some of the finest grass courts
around, they are still frustrating, especially after the
first week of play has done its damage. A few bad
bounces, one tough call, and a service break, and you're
out in the streets. Again, I take nothing away from
Bjorn's achievement; I am only saying that over the
course of five sets the superior player stands a far
better chance of winning on grass.

On grass you can possess limited skills and still be
a winner. If you've got a big serve and volley you are
officially dangerous—that your groundstrokes chase
the mailman will not cost you a grass-court match. On
grass the play is "come on in." You do not even need
a terrific volley. More often than not a short, dumpy
volley is as potent as the most slashing, well-delivered
volley you could think of. On grass the ball just slithers
and dies.

When you play on grass be sure to abbreviate your
backswings and be even more aware than usual of getting the racket face in a ready position early. This will
help you to reply to bad bounces, but do not get overly
sensitive of the possibility or you will lose your concentration and purpose. Whenever possible chip or
slice and come in, taking the ball as early as you can.
If the grass is slippery the attacking player is at a great
disadvantage, because she will not have the footing

necessary to launch a forward attack. I dislike wet grass intensely because I do not get to use my speed. Charging into the net on a wet grass court can be both dangerous and hilarious—players tend to hit the turf with unusual and embarrassing frequency. Pam Shriver is also well suited to grass. Shriver merely has to take one long stride and she can cover a lot of net. But if the court is slippery, mix it up. Use all of your spins, chops, slices and dices, lengths and speeds, and hit behind your opponent as much as you can, because changing directions is no simple task. If you've gotten your opponent off balance or on the run, get in there and finish the point.

Indoor Courts

In the past couple of years I have come to own the winter circuit, which is played indoors on carpet. It has been suggested to me that I enter the carpet business upon retirement because I already seem to have a fine knowledge and appreciation for it. This may be true, but it is not only the surface that I like so much. I love everything about the Great Indoors. You cannot ask for more controlled conditions, which would favor the best, most accurate player. Indoors I do not have to worry about the wind, the sun, too much cold, or too much heat. I can totally concentrate on my matches.

The synthetic courts play the way a perfect grass court would play. The ball stays low and keeps most of its pace, so slices and drives are encouraged. These courts favor the serve-and-volley player, but baseliners can get involved in long rallies as well, as long as they maintain good depth on their strokes. I use just about every shot I own when I play indoors, except for my kick serve, which I only use sparingly to break up a pattern and catch my opponent by surprise.

The surrounding area of indoor courts is generally smaller than the periphery of outdoor courts. Here's where you get to dust off all the angles you've got, the sharper the better. Angling your opponents wide on indoor courts is a great ploy because if the angle achieved is dramatic enough, your opponent will run out of court area to play the ball from. I know that my leftie serve takes on added meaning, especially to the ad court, where I like to try to send my opponent into the spectators' laps. By all means be clever and stretch your opponent beyond the boundaries of the indoor court.

The Mental Aspects of Tennis

Concentration

I never used to concentrate on concentrating. The way I had it figured was that whenever I really needed to settle down and focus in for the match, all I had to do was turn it on. It was not long after this cherished belief was shattered that I learned the ugly truth about the Easter Bunny being a phony. The point is, you can be out there in the middle of a tough match pleading to yourself, "Concentrate! Concentrate!" and it won't happen for you. Concentration is much more elusive than that.

Billie Jean King has spoken about what total concentration is like. "I can almost feel it coming," she says. "It usually happens on one of those days when everything is right, when the crowd is large and enthusiastic and my concentration is so perfect it almost seems as though I'm able to transport myself beyond the turmoil of the court to some place of total peace and calm. I know where the ball is on every shot, and it always looks as big and well-defined as a basketball. Just a huge thing I couldn't miss if I wanted to. I've got perfect control of the match, rhythms and movements are excellent, everything's in total balance. It's just an Aaaaaah."

Very few people ever get to know this feeling, but then again, few people have trained the way Billie Jean has, disciplining her body and mind to the point where she can achieve this incredible sense of harmony and understanding of the game. I know what Billie Jean speaks of—I have had matches like that as well. I have also lost carelessly because something caused my concentration to wane. It has been a distraction in the audience—someone yelling or shuffling around in the aisles. It has been a case of frazzled nerves in a high-pressure match that has allowed uninvited thoughts to surface. There have been times when I have relaxed my mind after gaining a large lead over my opponent. I would say to myself, "It's in the bag" and proceed to feel sorry for my soon-to-be-vanquished foe, letting up so as not to cause embarrassment. The wrong person would get embarrassed. Then, of course, there is *this* surefire way to lose concentration: Have a major problem or worry outside of the tennis court. All too often the problem will insist that it accompany you to your match, where it will sit next to you on changeovers, consult with you at the baseline, and nag you at the net. So what do you do at times like this?

Unfortunately, you can do very little at that stage. The concentration that you need has to come to you way before your match. Concentration is born on the practice court, along with your groundstrokes, your foot speed, and everything else. You must mentally treat your practice sessions as matches, concentrating on every ball you hit. Do not be thinking about your practice partner, your upcoming match, or anything else but your own game. You must be keen, alert, and enthused, and as you cover all of your shots, thinking about just one thing at a time, you are making the mental process more and more automatic. When you become a true craftsman at something, having spent long, intense hours of disciplined work, you stop wondering whether your hands will obey what your mind has asked for. It is something you no longer have to think about, because it is second nature to you. This is what a true tennis craftsman achieves. A better-quality practice creates a better-quality match.

I prepare mentally off the court, too. Especially if I've got a grudge match, or I want to prove something, win something big, I will go to sleep imagining what I am going to do. I try to envision the kind of points I want to be playing, the feeling of euphoria after the win, everything. Sometimes I have woken up the next day feeling like it's already happened. That's how real I can imagine the tennis to be.

In practice sessions be certain to do quickness drills, exercises that demand fast thinking and good reflexes. Also, perform drills that demand a minimum amount of balls to cross the net, and if you fail to reach that number, start again from zero. And, of course, practice playing sets against good players, and play to win. Concentration can become a habit. So can winning.

How to Practice Concentration

As I've mentioned, quick drills at the net will aid in prolonging your concentration efforts on the volley and will force you to focus in on the ball off your opponent's racket. Long baseline drills are also a good idea.

When I am training with Renee Richards, she will give me specific goals for varying periods of time—five minutes of balls into one corner, perhaps, and then a switch to the opposite end, or every ball past the service line for ten minutes. These drills intensify my concentration and purpose. Renee might also make the rules very specific. If she hits the ball deep into the court, my replies must all land as deep. If her ball bounces high, I must counter with a flat drive. If it's low, I must slice and come to net for the volley. Or she will stay in one corner of the baseline and run me all over the court, but I must play every ball directly back to her. She may stipulate that I must clear at least one hundred shots before the drill is over. Believe me, after the first sixty or seventy shots my concentration is running high, to say the least. These kinds of incentive drills sharpen my concentration more than anything else.

Practicing to Music

Every now and then when I want to relax, lose my inhibitions, and feel more fluid, I turn up the tunes and practice to music. I find that music loosens up my body and mind, and I have waltzed off many a musical practice with sting in my shots and a song in my heart. You should definitely check this out for yourself, especially if you tend to cramp up when you play, getting yourself all pinched and uptight over the game. To those of you who are music lovers, combine two of your favorite things and see how splendidly this duet performs. One note of caution: Do not disrupt neighboring courts with an excess of volume. Not everyone appreciates music. We all boogie to a different drummer.

Attitude

My attitude has been one of the biggest changes in my game, and I credit Nancy Lieberman for the vast improvement in my mental outlook, my work ethics, and the control of my emotions. I truly think that I handle myself in a much better fashion than I did a few years ago. Like John McEnroe, I expect a lot from myself, and when I get angry, I show it. Some players, like us, do, while others don't. One thing is for certain: I'll never give myself an ulcer from holding things in.

Chris Evert Lloyd and Tracy Austin are known for their infinite cool, for never letting things visibly upset them no matter how unjust a call or how poorly they played a ball. They will never let you peek at what's bothering them, so you can never be sure if they are bothered at all. That's a great attitude.

I cannot pull that one off, but my idea is to show my opponents just how relaxed and confident I am feeling, that I, not they, are controlling the match; I do not want my opponent to know that I am upset by something, but if that happens, I try to make my anger work for me. I do not want to be defeated by my own dour outlook. That has certainly happened to me in the past, and Pam Shriver's attitude has caused her to lose matches as well. We are both emotional, high-strung people. Sometimes, channeled correctly, this can be a great advantage. How many times has John McEnroe gotten totally aggravated about a call or a player's stalling or his own mistakes, only to step up to the line on the next point and serve an aggravated ace? I have great respect for anger that is controlled, and I think I have gained a lot of control lately. It is not easy. It shows great strength of character, and mine can stand to get better. Nancy says that I tend to put over this really hostile attitude out on the court, when at number one in the world I should instead be oozing with ease and confidence, and look ready and willing to play at all times.

As I said, that isn't easy for me. At the 1982 Toyota Series Championships final against Chris, my attitude cost me the first set. The match had become a very big deal. Although my 1982 record spoke for itself, there were people who thought that by beating me in this final Chris could be ranked number one. I did not agree at all, but the press had been building up the match all week long. The whole thing had made me very edgy, and it showed. Chris was serving the first set at 4–3, the game at 0–30. I hit a ball to her baseline and I was sure I'd caught the tape. Chris muscled the ball wide off the skid, but my shot was called out. It shouldn't have bothered me so much—I still had chances to break her serve—but the whole thing had unnerved me, and I just couldn't shake it off. I kept thinking of what should have or could have been, and I continued to fume for points and points afterward, causing me to lose the opening set. I bounced back, all right. The episode did not cost me the whole match. But a few years ago it could have. I have come a long way.

To be a better champion than I am right now, my attitude still must improve. This may not be the case with you. You may be gracious in both victory and defeat, and give the benefit of the doubt willing to the other player. You may never let up for one point and wouldn't think of dogging a match. Your attitude about work could already be a healthy one. Or maybe you just have to work on certain parts of your attitude, such as giving more to a practice session. If your outlook is positive, believe me, that's half the battle.

If you are naturally emotional, this is something you are going to have to work on, because learning a good attitude is not an overnight proposition. That is why a particular story about Bjorn Borg is hard for me to believe. The story goes that Bjorn had a terrific temper when he was younger. He was supposed to have been really emotional, throwing rackets and tantrums all over Sweden, until one day when his father caught his act and told Bjorn that if he kept it up he wouldn't be allowed to play tennis anymore. BOOM! Like that Bjorn cut it out. Now, maybe it happened like that, but I don't believe it, because I know Bjorn off the court, and he just is not that emotional a guy. In any case, he certainly has a style to admire.

I have faced the fact that I will never stop being an emotional tennis player, because I will never stop being an emotional person. But I am tired of losing matches to attitude problems, and it just isn't going to happen that way anymore. I still talk out loud too much sometimes, berating myself long after the fact, but Renee and Nancy have made me better and have convinced me that it is something you really can work on and improve. I try to forget the last point played and go on with the show. I may walk around a little bit, take an extra five or ten seconds to regain my composure, and then proceed. It is a gradual process, but with practice you can actually talk yourself into or out of things.

You can train yourself to handle all sorts of problems on the court by practicing all your shots for hours on end, so that when the moment comes when you must play a big forehand it is not something foreign and scary to you. You can physically take yourself through all of the possibilities in a match, so why not take yourself through the necessary mental processes as well? Renee has shown me how to practice this. She used to throw examples of match situations at me and then explain what I should do, how I should play them, both in terms of execution and mentally, such as play aggressively at break point up, defensively at break point down. She would also explain my opponent's tendencies, weaknesses, and personality to me so that I could anticipate her probable movements. These days Renee does not have to tell me what to do; instead, she asks me what to do in a given situation, and it forces me to think about my mental as well as physical attack. These mental exercises have made me much stronger. If something comes up in a match, I no longer feel angry or confused or embittered by the turn of events. I just pull everything in, breathe deeply, and play the next point.

The Killer Instinct

The killer instinct. Are you born with this? Can you develop it? Can your coach give it to you?

Being competitive and having a killer instinct are two different things. I have always been competitive in everything I do, and until very recently I have never had a killer instinct in anything I've done. There is a vast difference in wanting to beat an opponent and wanting to kill her—that is, really letting her have it, no holds barred, no free points—a real drubbing. When Nancy plays basketball, she plays with total killer instinct. She wants the opposing team to look bad, humiliated. Nancy wants to shut them down. Whenever I played anything I was content to win. What Nancy has instilled in me is the idea that I must never give my opponent the opportunity or reason to believe that they could win the match.

Watch Chris Evert Lloyd or Tracy Austin and you will see the killer instinct at work. They play every point all out, regardless of their lead, and refuse to give their opponents a chance to breathe life into their own chances. What hurt me early in my career was this lack of purpose. I can remember so many three-setters then that should have been straight sets, and so many losses that should have been victories. It was common for me to be up 6–0, 5–1, and proceed to ease things up. I would think I had the match won, lose my concentration, or feel sorry for my opponent, and suddenly I'd be involved in a tie breaker to decide the third set. That's where killer instinct shines. Killer instinct gives you the power to finish the match. When you've got someone down, killer instinct will tell you to beat them and get off the court.

I still think that while you can pick up some killer instinct along the way, it is still just that—an instinct, one you are either born with or not. I think it is a lot like natural talent—you've either got it or you don't. Look at Evonne Goolagong Cawley. She has all the natural talent in the world and no killer instinct, yet she is a wonderful champion. There are those who sigh when they watch Evonne play and say, "If only she had the killer in her! How much better she could be!" That may be true, but it isn't Evonne. It has got to come, ultimately, from within. You can develop it to a certain extent, as I have, but in the end you must truly believe what you are trying to feel about your opponent. At least that is what happens with me. But what is very important for young players to remember is that when you have them where you want them, you must mentally stay on top of them. You cannot give them the opportunity to think that they can come back and beat you. Hold fast to your leads and play every single point as if you mean it.

How to Handle
Winning and Losing

Ideally, you should treat both winning and losing the same way. Knowing that you have given it your best should be as satisfying as any win and as comforting as possible in the face of defeat. The reaction to a win or a loss has got to be balanced—for you, your coach, your parents—and the attitude should always be, "Let's learn from this match and make the next one better."

When I was younger and my power game had not yet jelled, I was constantly getting beaten by my peers. I was also a lot smaller than everyone else. I used to have to go up against kids who were two heads taller when I competed in the twelve-and-unders. I had plenty of 6–0, 6–0 losses, but they rarely got me down because I knew how I wanted to play and I believed in my style and my potential. I could have bagged the net game and stayed on the baseline like everyone else was doing with success, but one day, I hoped, my game would work. It took a lot of losses, but at fourteen I started making my mark, and all of those losses had taught me plenty. You must always keep your game in the proper perspective and always look into the future. Remember, the immediate future is not what is important. It is how you wish to play in the end that gets you through the rough spots.

Do not compare yourself to other players around you. Some may be much more physically developed than you are, or have been playing longer than you have. A loss to this person should not devastate you. Some players, such as Billy Martin, peak early, while others, such as Wendy Turnbull, peak late. If you are a serve-and-volley player and your baseline friends keep winning against you, do not despair. You may just have to work a little harder. If you are a baseliner who gets bullied around the court by net rushers, do not get disgusted and refuse to play against them. Instead, play them more often so that you get used to their pace and develop your passes. If you are a hard worker, practicing five hours a day, and you lose to a player who barely warms up before a match, again, do not compare yourself to this player. A parent should not scold one of her children for studying five hours for a test and bringing home a "C" and praise her other child, who aces courses without cracking a book. These comparisons are unhealthy and unfair, and no one should lay that kind of judgment on you, especially yourself. What is key is that you perform up to your potential.

You must learn from both your wins and your losses. When you win, go over the match in your mind and try to discern what you did right, what you could have done better, and what it took from you mentally to beat your opponent. Sometimes you can win a match and not have played well at all. This has happened to me a lot. I have walked off a win, happy and satisfied, only to have Nancy or Renee say to me, "What was *that* all about? Where was your mind? Your topspin passing shot? Your lob?" And, of course, they were right. I may not have put much work into the match and won it anyway. Whether I've won or lost, I hate it when people come up to me and tell me that I played great when I know in my heart that I didn't.

You have got to be your own critic, or have people around who will tell it like it is. It's the same with losing a match. There are so many ways to lose a match, and you must take apart your game to find out what had cost you. You could have made mental errors, tactical errors, or technical errors. You might have lost because your forehand broke down, or you played to the wrong side of the court, or you failed to apply the pressure at the right time. Maybe you were just too tired or too sick to win that day. Whatever it is, think about it after the match is over. You may uncover some very telling patterns that you had not realized before. Just the act of putting the match in perspective may help you to sleep better that night.

Reviewing a match helps me immeasurably. Sometimes it takes a while before I honestly come to grips with a loss. I may sometimes have a problem admitting I goofed up a match. Renee will start to say something critical, and I will immediately say, "No, no, no." But five minutes later I'll admit to being wrong, and we'll talk. Deep down, of course, I'll have known immediately that what was said had been the truth, but just as deep down I would not immediately have been ready for the harsh reality of the loss. You may be the same way. Sometimes a little breathing room from the loss is all it takes before you can take on the criticism.

Parents and coaches have to be very careful in their treatment of a player's wins or losses. Some parents are all over their kids for losing, or spoil them rotten for bringing home a win. Coaches can be guilty of doing the same thing, and it can really beat up a kid emotionally. My father used to get on my case. Parents and coaches can get in the way too much and place the wrong amount of importance on key issues, thus destroying the "try" in the child and the love she has for the game. On the tour we've got a couple of parents running around who are just maniacs. They turn their kids into head cases, butting them up against the rest of the tour players, pushing them into too many tournaments when they are down or hurt or tired. There are plenty of players you do not hear about because they have become tennis casualties.

There must be plenty of support and respect all the way around, no matter how the scoreboard reads in the end. Athletes have very delicate psyches. A win should not make them uppity and superior, a loss should not bruise egos or cause a drop in self-esteem. All we are talking about is a game.

Guts

To be a gutsy player you must have a lot of discipline. You have got to be willing to stay out on the court, to scrape and lunge and dive for the ball no matter what the situation. You have to play your hardest even when you know that you are not playing your best. To my mind, "gutsing out a match" does not happen in the grand arenas like Wimbledon. At Wimbledon there is no question that you are 100 percent willing to win. Lack of nerve is what affects players at Wimbledon, not lack of guts. The gutsy matches I have won are the ones that no one hears about. They may be against someone like Mima Jausevec, a talented Yugoslavian player who is constantly flirting with the Top Ten rankings. Mima may be putting together a real fine game, and I could be way off mine, and it is in these situations that I get truly tested for guts.

I have more discipline than I've ever been given credit for, but there are times when I have not come through. In the 1982 Avon Championships final against Sylvia Hanika I was up a set and leading three games to one in the second. Sylvia began to play all out, and as she surged, my game dipped about 10 percent lower —certainly not so much that I couldn't have pulled through. But I never shook her off, I never pumped myself up enough to finish the match, and by the third set I was no longer playing to win, I was playing not to lose.

Against Chris Evert Lloyd in the 1982 Australian final it was a slightly different case. I had gone down there with a bad attitude—sort of listless and uncaring. I spoke to Nancy during the week and she said,

"What's wrong with you, anyway? It's the Australian Open." But I didn't get myself up, and during the finals I felt like I was just going through the motions. Don't ask me why, but I just didn't have it. The funny thing is, Nancy knew before I even left for Australia. It was evident in my practice sessions, my attitude, and my general washed-out spirit. Nancy is so disciplined that she would have found some way to win. We spoke about it a lot after I got back, and I understand now that if you do not demand a high level of self-discipline all of the time, you cannot expect to have guts all the time, either. It's a good lesson to learn.

Sportsmanship

In the same way that a player's personality can shine through on a tennis court, her character can as well, and not only when she loses. If there is one thing worse than being a bad loser, it's being a bad winner. Bad winners are the types who will give the impression of arrogant control upon defeating you, depriving you of your self-respect. Bad winners shout for joy upon match point, jump up and down, squeal, yell, the whole scene. Bad winners talk about their feats often and with great relish. Bad winners are a pain in the neck. The "Do unto others" rule really applies here. You must feel your own joy but be conscious of your vanquished opponent's sorrow. I will never forget how Pam Shriver acted upon defeating me at both the U.S. Opens that we met in. The first victory occurred when she was just fifteen years old, and she had just scored one of the most astonishing upsets in U.S. Open history. You would never have known it by watching Pam. When the last point was over, she didn't scream, she didn't jump or yell—she walked calmly to the net, mindful of my disappointment, and shook my hand. That was it. To have that kind of poise and control at fifteen was pretty impressive. And when Pam stopped my quest for a Grand Slam by beating me in the quarter-finals in 1982, it was the same thing, though we were by then good friends and very close. I hated to lose, but if I had to lose to any player, I was glad it was someone like Pam.

What about the bad losers? I don't have to tell you what they are all about. They are the whiners, the complainers, the cheaters, the ones with the great excuses. To hear them tell it, bad losers have never actually lost a match—it was somehow stolen from them, taken away by a lucky opponent, prejudiced linesmen, deathly illnesses. These people have never heard of a code of honor. They would never give someone the benefit of the doubt on a call. They will certainly not recognize their opponent's superior play. They may be just fine off the court—a good friend, a fun person, sincere. But once they step out on the court to play a match, their good qualities vanish. That is when you can tell who's who, really—when the pressure is on.

Some players will do anything to win, use any scam to disturb their opponents. It can be that they stall continually, have frequent outbursts, pick fights with the linespeople, bounce the ball fifteen times before they serve it. Some players will do anything to get the edge. To my mind that's not part of the game. Years ago I watched Billie Jean King play against a young Russian player, Natasha Chmeryova. I will never forget this match. It was at Eastbourne, England, the warm-up tournament for Wimbledon, and Billie was on court there with this talented teenager. She was talented in more than just tennis. After a while it became obvious that she was going for an Oscar with her performance. I am pretty sure she was playing "Camille," because it looked like she could be close to death at any time. The hilarious part of it was that Natasha would be doubled over with seemingly agonizing cramps one minute, and running like a gazelle the very next point. That sort of thing can be unnerving to say the very least. And Billie Jean would look up every now and then and say to the players who were watching, "What is this?" What it was was a form of cheating.

Your emotions should never lead you to this form of gamesmanship. It could be that you place too much emphasis on winning, no matter the cost, or perhaps you are getting that pressure from your parents. It's okay to be confident, but not to be cocky and abusive. There was more gentility to the game when I was growing up. Now there is a pervading attitude that you are either the best or nothing, and it can create a tremendous conflict inside of you. You must try not to let it bother you if your opponent adopts this attitude, and try not to let it happen to you at all cost. People will think a lot more of you, and not just on the tennis court.

Doubles

If you are like me, you love tennis and you love team sports. Doubles is both of these, and more often than not, at any tournament the best, most exciting tennis comes out of a doubles match.

I have had much success in doubles, and with various partners. In fact, I qualified for the 1980 Tournament of Champions doubles three different times and with three different players—I won the Australian Open with Betsy Nagelsen, Amelia Island with Pam Shriver, and Wimbledon with Billie Jean King. I have also won titles with Candy Reynolds, Anne Smith, Olga Morozova, Rosie Casals, Betty Stove, and Janet Newberry. Since 1981 I've been playing with Pam Shriver almost exclusively, and we are the best doubles team in the world these days, but my own feeling is that if Billie Jean King were in her prime right now, we would be the greatest team of all time.

As a doubles player Billie is still awesome. She is the smartest doubles player ever, for one thing. She also has all the shots and all the guts, and when we won the Wimbledon doubles in 1979, her twentieth title there, it was one of the most exciting moments of my life. There was so much pressure that day. I was more nervous for that match than for any singles match I've ever played. Billie Jean and I got along really well. I have never had any real problems getting along and communicating with my partners because I know their personalities and adjust accordingly. Pam, for instance, is easier to talk to when we're losing than Billie Jean was because Pam just keeps communicating and relating to what is happening. We are constantly helping each other with ideas, especially if we are in trouble. Anne Smith, on the other hand, is a lot more quiet and doesn't like to get chatty out there, whatever the score is. Understanding your partner, adjusting to suit each other's needs, and maintaining a positive attitude at all times are necessary, especially if you intend to play with the same partner again. There have been many times when either Pam or myself was playing subpar doubles, and we'd be there for each other, two friends working as a team. If I would be playing badly, she would try to compensate and take more shots or calm me down or psyche me back up—whatever I needed to pull through. I would say to her, "Well, I owe you one there." We always feel like there's no problem as long as we both keep trying. I tried for Billie Jean at Wimbledon, and Pam sure tried hard for me at the 1981 U.S. Open. I had lost to Tracy Austin in the final of the singles, and Pam and I had to play against Rosie Casals and Wendy Turnbull less than two hours later in the doubles semifinals. I was still devastated from my loss to Tracy, and Pam wanted so much to win the doubles for me. When we lost I think that Pam was even more upset than I was. That's the kind of person she is and the kind of doubles player she is. A bond forms in team sports that is unique and special, making the wins and losses memorable and touching in a way that an individual sport just can't match. Everyone should play doubles.

What Makes a Good Doubles Player

Simply put, a good doubles player must serve, volley, and return serve well. Any weakness in one of these three areas will hurt the team and undoubtedly get picked on by smart opponents. If your serve or your partner's serve is not big, it should at least be consistent and well placed, allowing for an easier first volley. If someone has a weak volley, a lot of the sting comes out of the team, and it is important to compensate by hitting low and hard from the baseline. If you are not the kind of player who really tags the return of serve, again, make it consistent and well placed. Power does not necessarily make a good return. In fact, many top teams have a power returner and a placement returner, and this makes things difficult for the opposing team because they face two totally different balls on their first return.

A good doubles player should show quickness at net. Good reflexes count heavily in doubles, where the pace can become brutally fast, and decisiveness is paramount. Good doubles players understand how to utilize the nine extra feet of court that the side alleys bring to doubles. Taking the net with drop shots, lobs, drives, and by angling well all over the court are what make doubles so interesting and exciting.

I find that there are not that many two-handed

backhand players or confirmed baseline players who can be part of a successful doubles team. A big problem two-handed backhanders face is that their reach is limited and their backhand volleys are generally weaker than a one-handed backhand player's volleys. Strict baseline players have the problem of approaching the net with confidence, although if their strength is from the baseline, that is where they should position themselves. Baseliners also tend to clear the net by a great margin on their shots, and any kind of good doubles team will beat up on such height. Sometimes two backcourt players together make a very tough team because they stay on the baseline and refuse to make errors, sending everything back and daring the opposing team to put away the ball. But, in general, doubles is won at the net, so someone with a nose for the net can be a valuable doubles partner.

A good doubles player is a good team player, thoughtful, unselfish, and possessing a positive attitude and kind demeanor. The compatibility of two game styles is also important in doubles, but even more important is the compatibility of the two players as a working, caring team. Not all people think this way, but I feel it is very important that you like your partner. A doubles team is a lot like a regular relationship between two people. There has got to be deep respect and good feeling for each other, or else the team will break down in bad times, when you need unity the most. If you can mesh both your personality and your game with your partner's, you will be a good team player on a strong team.

Why am I a particularly good doubles player? First

of all, I love playing on a team. Second, my ability to adjust to a partner's game or a tough situation is intuitive and automatic. My hand–eye coordination is acutely developed, as are my reflexes, which are more like a man's than a woman's. In doubles it helps to have a strong upper body and wrist for power volleying, and I've got both. Most of all I think I have a quick and facile mind and a playful, creative attitude about playing the game of doubles. It comes very naturally to me.

The Cardinal Rules of Doubles

Play the Percentages

Make sure that you maintain a high percentage of first serves, returns of serves, and volleys. If this means that you must serve at three-quarter pace, do just that. If you enjoy pounding your returns but they are not finding the court with regularity, pull back on the pace and concentrate on accuracy. Give your opponents a chance to play the ball, and go for the winner only when you have set yourself up. Keep your first volleys deep until you draw a weak enough reply to put away the ball. Avoid the cutesy dink volleys and the dramatic angles when a firm and well-placed shot will do.

Keep the Ball in Front of You

This will not only allow for more control, touch, pace, and disguise, but also you will be robbing your opponents of time if you take the early ball.

Use All of the Shots

In doubles more than singles you will need to employ your drop shots, lobs, stop volleys, and all your other change-up strokes. Sometimes a lob can win a point much easier than a drive, and sometimes a shot down the middle of the court is more effective than the cagiest angle. Use all of your shots and a lot of imagination.

Communicate with Your Partner

This is true at all times in a match. It will keep you looser, more relaxed, and it lets your opponents know that you are working together as a team. If you feel as though your team should try something different or concentrate on one particular player, mention it to your partner. If you are not playing well and have lost your confidence, tell her that as well, and she can then try to play more shots or rework strategy. If you feel that your partner is playing something the wrong way, bring that up too, but make sure that it is in a way that does not undermine the team spirit. Positive feedback builds the team's confidence and makes playing together a lot more enjoyable. Keep communicating when your team is losing—don't get down and stop talking.

Keeping Your Opponents Honest

If your shots are too patterned in doubles, your opponents will take more and more poaching chances. It's a good idea to shoot a ball down the netman's alley early in a match to keep that player from becoming too bold. Likewise, you should be doing a lot of moving around on your side of the net so that your opponents cannot establish a winning attitude about returning serve. I have seen a few early poaches in the beginning of the first set make some teams tentative for the entire match. So shake up your opponents while demanding that they keep their act clean.

Faking is great, too. A fake poach is when you move early enough for your opponent to detect your intent, then get back to your original position to intercept their pass. I have gotten into my fakes a lot lately, I think from playing so much basketball. In that sport there are head fakes, body fakes, feints to the left and right, every kind imaginable. I've brought a couple of those moves to the tennis court, and I have even started double faking lately, a move that has my partner, Pam, looking on in mock horror. The first time I pulled it was one of my most satisfying moments, to be sure. You shouldn't go crazy on the faking business, but try a few fakes and have a good time with them.

If You Poach the Ball, Put It Away

A poached ball should not come back to you. A poach is meant to be aggressive and decisive, and any kind of reply means almost certain loss of the point. A mispoach leaves the court wide open on one side. The poach is the last word in the point, so do not move indecisively. And once you bolt, don't turn back— attack, which means your partner needs to cover for you and move over to your side of the court.

Break up the Opposing Team

Try to destroy the unity of the opposing team by hitting down the center of the court, ganging up on the weaker player, and exploiting every possible weakness the team might have. All things being equal, the better "team" should win the close ones. Make sure that it is your team.

Cover for Each Other

Don't get locked into "your" side of the court. If a lob has got your team on the run and your partner can field the ball better than you, cross and guard her territory to close up the hole in the court. If you can shag down a drop volley on your partner's side better than she, yell for the ball and run to it, your partner assuming your position. When you move, think in terms of a team.

Play Balls Down the Center

This is one of the best doubles strategies and one of the least used. A shot hit down the center denies opponents an angle to work off of, can cause confusion and uncertainty as to who should play it, and is a simpler shot to hit. Just remember that when you play down the center, the shot must be forcefully hit or else it will be defensive. Really give the ball a ride and use angles on the follow-up shots.

Lob High and Deeply

On defensive lobs, the type you throw up when you
have lost your court position and need time to regain
it, it is always better to lob too long than too short.
A too-short lob will be put away, but a too-long lob
may get mistakenly played and keep you into the point.
When you lob you should aim for your opponents' baseline, not the center of the court. An offensive lob generally has a bit of topspin, and as long as it flies over
your opponents' racket heads, it does not have to be
that high. The topspin will make the lob shoot away
from your opponents on the bounce, so that spin, along
with the relatively low height over the net, will give
your opponents a very tough time to get the ball back.

Let the Stronger Server Serve First

The partner who has an easier time holding serve
should obviously serve first for every set. Remember,
teams can switch the order of serving for every new
set. Be mindful of which server gets the sun and the
wind to contend with.

Play a Lot of Balls Cross-Court

You want to avoid the player at net, and you also want
to keep your partner in good position, so most of the
time return serve and rally cross-court. Going for the
occasional line is a good idea if you are not leaving
huge gaps in the court by doing so. Even when you
are returning a lot of cross-courts, mix up the pace and
angle of the returns to make the server's first volley a
more difficult task.

Move Together as a Team

When your partner poaches and is obviously not going back to her side, you better make sure that you get over there fast in case your opponents get the ball back. Always cover up for your partner. Also, move backward and forward as a team. If a lob is hit over your partner's head, and she has to go back for it, you have to get back as well. Chances are your partner will have to hit a lob, making you an easy target at the net. By the same token, when you are both back, you should move forward together, eliminating "holes" on your side of the court so that your opponents will not have any easy winners.

How to Pick Which Side to Play On

The most common rule you hear for doubles is, "Let the stronger player take the ad court." The reasoning behind this rule is that the important points—the 15–30, ad points, and break points—are played to the ad side of the court and should be handled by the better player. Another common rule is, "The leftie takes the ad court." This is because a leftie would be taking the serves to her forehand side, and there would be two forehands covering the alleys as well. Both of these rules are valid but are hardly carved in stone.

My feeling is that you should play on whichever side feels more comfortable to you. The points played on the deuce side of the court can be just as important as those played on the ad side. Some people have weak backhand returns of serve. If that is the case, that person should assume the deuce court. A player with a good backhand volley will be strong playing from the deuce side, and if she's got a big forehand she will get to power her returns from there, whereas the backhand side would rob her of her strength. If one of the players is more mobile than the other, she should play the ad side, where she will be able to poach forehand volleys with confidence. It's all so individual. Pam Shriver and I play the deuce-ad court, and it works well for us. At the time when we first hooked up as a team, Pam liked the backhand side as much as I did, but we decided to try it with me as a leftie taking the ad court. Not only are we able to utilize my left-handedness on the alleys, but also both of our strengths, our backhand volleys, are down the middle of the court, where more balls are played anyway. This makes for a solid and imposing team. It takes two fine doubles players to beat us.

The Australian (or "I") Formation

I have rarely used or played against the Australian, or "I," formation. As a matter of fact, the last time I remember a women's team using the Australian formation was years ago when Mona Guerrant and Greer Stevens would effectively utilize this option.

The "I" formation is the positioning of players so that the server's partner stands on the same side of the court as the server. The time to use this formation is when you are serving to a player who is returning extremely tough grooved shots. This positioning will force the returner to hit into the other, less comfortable court. It is also an effective way to couch a weakness on the serving team. If you have a weak serve and a good forehand, for instance, you can serve to the ad court and then cover your own deuce court, making your opponent avoid the netman and play right into your strength. If you want to try this, you should practice with your partner first, because suddenly changing your court coverage may make you a little bit confused and slow to the ball. The really beautiful aspects of the "I" formation are that it can shoot a surprise into your opponents and draw errors and that you can go from the "I" back to the normal positioning at any time in the match.

Mixed Doubles

Ideally there should be no real difference between doubles and mixed doubles. If the woman is a good doubles player, she will be a good mixed doubles player, unless she can be intimidated by the extra power of men's shots. If this is not the case, she should hold her own just fine and concentrate on the same basic tenets of good doubles—holding serve, making consistent returns, and volleying well.

Patterns tend to develop in mixed doubles. For instance, the man is usually responsible for more of the court than the woman because of his speed and reach, and the questionable down-the-middle shots are generally fielded by the guy. (This holds true for lobs and drop shots as well.) But this is not to say that the woman should be intimidated out of holding up her end of the deal. I have seen Billie Jean King call for overheads plenty of times in mixed doubles, and she can volley as well as any man out there. I feel just as capable, too. Just as in regular doubles, play the side of the court that makes your team work best. When I played mixed doubles with Dennis Ralston, he took the ad court even though he had always played the deuce side and I had always liked the ad side. We were following the "mixed doubles rule," and it was a big mistake. We'd have been much tougher the other way around.

Practice with your partner or some other men before you play any mixed doubles so that you can get used to the accelerated speed and the heaviness of a man's strokes. The element of surprise figures big in mixed doubles, because many men assume that you will keep the ball away from them at all cost. Shoot some down their alleys every now and then, or volley right at their feet when they would least expect it. And maintain a constant dialogue with your partner, even after you have gotten to know each other's game well.

How Doubles Can Help Singles

When people ask John McEnroe and me why we play so much doubles on top of our singles play, we each tell them the same thing. Apart from the enjoyment of playing on a team and using different strategy, doubles helps singles play in many ways. The quickness of doubles—the volleys and brief exchanges—helps to make me faster and sharper in singles. I react quicker to situations, find interesting shots, and explore many more angles that I can carry over into my singles. Doubles play puts a high premium on serving and volleying well, which is the foundation for my singles game, and the constant pressure to make a forceful first volley in doubles is a key tactic and often undervalued in singles. In doubles I always expect the ball to come back. So often in singles I was guilty of thinking I'd hit a winner, and the point would not have been over at all. Doubles keeps you riveted to the point until its conclusion, a good habit to get into for the potentially overconfident player.

More personally, I enjoy doubles because being part of a team takes the pressure off. When I lose in singles at any tournament it undoubtedly makes the headlines the next day, but a loss in doubles is far less traumatic, so I don't have to bear the heavy burden of coming through every time I walk out to play a match. Doubles is a lighter load because that is how many people perceive the doubles action in a tournament. I also feel much more involved, more "into" a tournament, if I am in both events. The few times that I entered just the singles or lost early in doubles have been terrible, because on the day of the finals I watched the match and felt like I'd missed out on something good. On a subconscious level I am better able to concentrate in singles if I am doing double duty and playing doubles. I just take myself more seriously.

Coaching

I have not had many coaches at all. My stepfather got me out on the court first, and when he was working with me there was hardly ever a shot I'd make that he didn't have something to say about. And it was always something I'd done wrong. It drove me up a wall, because he would stop play and show me my shot in slow motion, exaggerating how badly it was executed. But I've got to admit that his method worked because he gave me most of the strokes in my game and I am as technically sound as anybody. After my stepfather worked on my game, a great Czech coach named George Palma took an active interest in me and improved everything, especially my backhand. I had been using both hands to swing, and George explained how this was choking my reach, so I switched to a one-handed stroke. By the time I was twelve years old, I was basically on my own. I was a natural athlete and a natural serve-and-volley player, and as the years went by I became more and more proficient at my style of play.

I was gifted enough to get by. When I first started to play tennis in the United States, both Billie Jean King and Rosie Casals showed interest in my game and helped me a bit. But I was used to playing on a strictly instinctive basis, so why should I have trained any harder? And within a few years I had realized my dream of becoming number one. My reaction was to sit back and relax. I sat back and lost.

Luckily for me, I met Nancy Lieberman when I did. I was at a low ebb—almost no confidence or direction—and she turned my head around about desire, motivation, and the will to win. A few months later, I hooked up with Renee Richards, and she brought all the missing parts to my game. I am emotional, volatile, and explosive, while Renee is just the opposite. She has a calculating mind, an intellectualization, a cold approach to the game. But it's even more than a technical and intellectual outlook that Renee gives to me. It's actually very subtle. There is a lot of psychology and emotion involved. Renee says that I am like a racehorse. It takes a lot to get me into the gate and ready to run. I've got to get into the right frame of mind. Renee and Nancy get me there.

What Coaching Has Done for My Game

As I've said, for most of my life I played on instinct and intuition. I had one basic concept—get to the net at all cost. There was no way I was going to hang back and rally from the baseline, even if my opponent did possess a fine return of serve and a strong passing shot. Renee taught me when to serve and volley and when to stay back.

Renee also taught me when really to go for my returns and when not to, and how to threaten my opponent from the backcourt. I had been neglecting the weaponry of my forehand on the ad side of the court. Renee showed me how important it was to run around my backhand on the break points and really go for a forehand biggie. It's terrific, because it intimidates my opponents and can even draw double faults. Conversely, Renee stopped my habit of running around for a forehand on the deuce side, because that move took me well off the court, leaving plenty of room for my opponent to play into.

With Renee I have built up my baseline game to the point where I have the confidence to stay back until I get the short ball. I no longer feel any of that panic and anxiety at the baseline. It's not such a spooky place after all. I use the whole court better now.

Renee is a great student of the game and its players and knows every player's strengths and weaknesses. She has notebooks full of player information—their pet shots, their patterns and strategies, their past performances against me. The night before I play a match Renee will review my opponent, going over old matches, what she is likely to do against me, and what I should do against her. This process used to take about forty-five minutes to run through, but at this stage I can talk to Renee for just a few minutes and I'm ready for the next day. I have learned from her how to do the work myself. The next day I will practice (with Renee if I play a leftie), and we will review once more what will happen in the match. Once I walk on the court there is no more communication. Renee doesn't signal me or say words of encouragement or anything—she is a presence I like, and for me that's enough in a match.

On the practice court Renee is anything but silent. Besides changing my one-game-plan tactics, which took a lot of explaining, she worked a lot on technique. I made one glaring technical error all the time—my big-swinging forehand volley, the shot that many people consider cost me the 1981 U.S. Open against Tracy Austin. Renee worked on my technique, the angle of my racket, all of my options with the shot. Now it's solid. We worked on my forehand, because I had always had a rather flat delivery. We put a lot more roll on it, the kind that does not go away under pressure but only gets stronger. I can hit harder than ever and gain control in the process.

She helped my backhand side as well. My footwork was not as good on my backhand as on my forehand, which I hadn't realized. It made it difficult for me to drive the ball and pass with confidence. We worked hard to develop a topspin backhand, and I use it all the time.

I even let Renee change my serve, although it had always worked well for me. I had the same serving technique as John Newcombe, rocking backward, then forward, yet I had no real thrust. We changed my stance to a dead-even balance, slightly more closed, and I learned to spring up into the ball more. My tosses used to reveal my intent, but now I toss the ball into the same spot for each serve, giving nothing away. Renee taught me when to use the different serves, too. One of my biggest technical fallacies was decelerating on my strokes to gain more control. This, of course, had the opposite effect—I was losing control by trying to hold in the stroke. We worked on finishing the strokes, the idea of expanding rather than contracting, and it is the extension that gives me the control I was seeking. All of these were very important lessons for me to learn. Coupled with Nancy's drive and enthusiasm, I began to look at the game of tennis in an entirely different light. I needed good coaching and a lot of motivation before I could realize my potential.

How to Choose a Coach

Before you begin to look for a coach you should have in mind the type of coaching you personally require. Do you need a lot of technical work on your game? Are you weak on strategy? On self-discipline? Hopefully you can find someone strong in each of these areas, but you must know that coaches, like players, have their own style and theories, and some place more importance on one particular area than on others.

Know that your personalities will interact with one another. Some coaches are yellers—loud and aggressive, with lots of feedback. Some coaches are quiet and mellow and hardly say a word. There are coaches who rarely pass compliments and really shovel the criticism, which is not my scene at all. That kind of negative-reinforcement routine never did the trick for me. My stepfather was like that. But it could be what you need to get going. People's needs are different.

A good coach must be very perceptive concerning the athlete. He must know you like a book and understand your moods and feelings. He should be able to tell whether you are down on your game or just having a lazy day or if you're tired or sick, and deal with it accordingly, telling you to take a rest or get down to work.

A good coach can dissect your game and decide what is good and bad about it, and how to develop both the strengths and weaknesses. He must know how much work should be devoted to each. He must calculate just how much he should change a stroke, and how much he should experiment in accordance with your tournament schedule. You should never feel a loss of confidence in your coach, and he should instill that kind of confidence in you. He should not try to bluff you by telling you how well you're playing if that just isn't the case. The worst thing is to get hooked in with a coach who just keeps complimenting your progress when there really hasn't been a change at all. That coach is lazy and not doing the job asked of him.

You must find a coach you trust and respect. I have a tremendous amount of respect and faith in what Renee tells me. She keeps the game simple for me and never gets me confused by giving me too many technical considerations to worry about at one time. Renee gets me feeling good about my game, and Nancy gets me motivated and psyched to the point where I am confident, even cocky to some extent. I walk onto the court with a certain aura about me that I would not have been able to create myself. A good coach can give you the things you cannot give yourself.

Coaching is different in tennis than in all other sports. In basketball, for instance, a player can call a time-out, consult with his coach, and turn the entire game around. That is a great luxury that tennis does not enjoy. A tennis coach can only walk you as far as the court. After that you are on your own. All of the coaching has to come beforehand.

Before you pick a coach, observe his style of teaching. Ask others who have taken lessons from him what he is like to work with. If you like his style, go to him and stay with him. Do not bounce from pro to pro, because their varying styles of coaching may easily confuse and frustrate. One coach at a time can best understand your game and gauge your progress.

The Coaching Computer

Robert Haas, the man who programmed my nutritional needs, and an associate of his have designed and programmed a tennis computer that I have used from time to time. The computer is fed an entire tennis match about thirty times, analyzing and breaking down the points stroke by stroke until previously unseen patterns become evident. What we look for in this breakdown are my patterns and those of my opponent. We find tendencies. Perhaps one top player will continually hit a return to the same spot at break point, or hit the ball harder, or perhaps slice more when down. What the computer has pointed up is that when the pressure is on, players stay true to their tendencies, and this knowledge is helpful against patterned players such as Chris Evert Lloyd and Tracy Austin. By understanding both my game and that of my opponent, I feel as though I have a far clearer insight into what my future matches might hold. The computer is a good, accurate scout.

Some Other Tennis Tips

How to Use the Warm-up Time Efficiently

In the pros we are given five minutes to warm up for the match. At the country club or the park, the scene is considerably more relaxed. I have seen club players warm up for about an hour before they finally decide to play out some points. Or there will be a doubles match going on, and after all the groundstrokes and volleys are squared away, one person will serve the game, taking four or five practice serves before he raises the balls and says, "These are good." After he's done serving, the opposite side will choose a server, and again the practice swings begin. When the last ball finds the service box, that guy is ready to serve. Once, I saw two guys come out to play on the court right next to where I was practicing. One of the players walked on the court with his racket in one of those old wooden frames, which sort of tipped me off this man had not done his fair share of tennis playing in the past. This same man proceeded to walk to the base-line with two balls in his hand and he just cracked two serves as hard as he could. No warm-up, no stretching, not even a friendly groundstroke or two. It was hilarious.

When you are given five minutes in which to warm up, spend the first few minutes hitting your groundstrokes, and concentrate well on moving your feet. Move then to the net area for some volleys and overheads. Your opponent will then come up and take her volleys and overheads. In the two remaining minutes you should take your serves, and remember to take them from both the deuce and the ad side of the court, hitting both your first and second serves.

So much for the warm-up directly preceding the match. Ideally you should practice anywhere from thirty minutes to an hour at some point before the match and get grooved on your shots and acclimated to the playing conditions. That way the five minutes serve as a tune-up. You should be totally warmed up physically—stretched, blood pumping, muscles ready to perform.

I take a forty-five-minute warm-up before my matches. During that time I go through every shot I've got. I must hit the entire assortment because I use all of my strokes in my matches. I will start on the baseline and take my time with my groundstrokes, experimenting with spins, length, and pace. I will then come to the net, hit some easy volleys, and then stretch out on some tough ones. Then I will go through the other motions—hitting approach shots, putting away volleys, practicing my overheads, dinking some drop shots, hitting high and low volleys. I will then have my practice partner run through the same things, with me responding to her approaches, volleys, and drop shots.

I will practice certain drills—one where I must run down a drop shot, then a lob, hit first serves and come in, hit second serves and stay back. I try to create possible match situations and practice all the conceivable responses. There should be no surprises in a match, never a time when you say to yourself, "Oh, no! I didn't hit any of them today." Believe me, you will always get the shot you hadn't practiced that day. That does not happen much anymore with me. I never used to practice my lobbing or my second serve, but now that has become automatic. Prepare for the match completely, as though you are going to school, as if the match is a test. Because it actually is one.

Taking Lessons

No matter what your level of play or interest in tennis, taking lessons is good for you. I don't know anyone who goes out on the court and doesn't care whether or not they improve. You can derive far more pleasure out of the game if you play it correctly and practice with purpose. The thing I see most is the business of playing far too many sets and taking far too few lessons. Yet in a one-hour tennis lesson you will hit four times the amount of balls you'd have hit in an hour of set playing. As boring as drills may be, the constant repetition of a correct stroke is what gives you confidence in it. A pro can control your shots, feed you exactly what you need to work on, and analyze your stroke production. Perhaps you play with a faulty grip, or perhaps you are gripping the racket too tightly. Your footwork may be slow, or your swing inefficient. If you want to add new dimensions to your game or correct old habits that lose you matches, stop playing sets and return to the practice court. That's what I do.

Lefties

In case you haven't noticed, I am a leftie, and I consider myself lucky to be one. The potential advantages of being left-handed are great. I was fortunate that early in my life no one tampered with my natural inclination and guided the racket into my other hand. That very thing happened to Ken Rosewall. As a young boy Ken played left-handed tennis, but the people who watched him would not accept the idea and taught him to play from the other side instead. Margaret Court was a born leftie as well, but when she saw all the people around her playing with the opposite hand, she too switched. Who knows how well these two could have played as lefties, considering how devastating they were with their other hand?

There are far fewer lefties than righties in this world, which gives us lefties many headaches in situations where an item obviously was designed for a right-handed person. But on a tennis court we have the advantage right away. A player who is well versed in her own patterns of play must reverse her typical strategies when facing a leftie. Many people develop rhythms and pet shots, such as a favorite lob to one side of the court or serving the ball to a certain corner. So if a player's favorite ploy is to go cross-court on her backhand to her opponent's backhand side, she will find that her left-handed opponent doesn't have a backhand over there—that side is to her forehand. To get to her opponent's backhand she would then have to resort to her seldom-used down-the-liner, not the shot that brings home the bacon. This can be a stressful situation, the way that trying to use scissors designed for a rightie can be a stressful situation for a left-hander. Welcome to the world of discomfort that these revelations bring, and then, of course, learn how to make the best of it.

The biggest advantage a leftie has is on her serve, which takes on the opposite spin of a right-hander's delivery. Even a baseline leftie like Stacy Margolin has a pretty tough slice serve that sends her opponents off the court. Barbara Potter and myself have big leftie swings, serves that do a lot of our talking for us in a match. Of course, after several games have gone by, your opponent will have gotten the chance to accustom herself to your delivery and may have figured out how to combat it. That is why it is important to use your leftie advantage wisely, or you lose it. My spin serves off the court are vital to my game, but I will also spin them directly at my opponent's body, especially if the serves are big, thereby denying them any angle or muscle into the return. If my opponent is short I will put in my sliders that can stretch her off the court and out of position. If my opponent is not quick I will feint off a very shallow spin that is tough to chase down. And, of course, I will pump in the biggies too, especially down the "T." Another good serve for a leftie to employ is a kicker down the deuce, for the opponent will be forced to reply to a seldom-seen high backhand.

When you must play against a leftie, try to get some practice against a southpaw beforehand. Be conscious of the difference in the leftie spins, and get used to changing your patterns and pet shots. Do not forget, for example, that your normal lob over an opponent's backhand will be landing right into your leftie opponent's strength. If you want to avoid eating unnecessary fuzz, move your lob over to the other side in practice so that you will remember it for the match. Move very quickly to the ball. It will be bouncing away from you a lot, particularly on your returns of serve.

Leftie Doubles

Some of the best doubles combinations ever, such as Rod Laver and Roy Emerson, were leftie-rightie combinations. There is a common rule when playing with a leftie (I like to think of it as playing with a rightie) that says, "The leftie takes the ad court." I do not believe that this should be a set rule. I happen to like playing the ad side, and Pam Shriver likes playing the deuce side, and that is why we play that way. We both return serve better off our respective halves of the court. I feel as though I come into the net better on the ad side, too. I slice my backhand and charge in tight, something that many lefties do well, or hit my forehand and do the same. On the deuce side a leftie has a longer way to run off a backhand return, whereas to a rightie that is a wide forehand, a shot many of them like to hit. But Laver and Emmo played it just the opposite, and very effectively, too. Although they had to face the prospect of having two wide backhand returns, they were deadly down the middle with their two big forehand volleys, making it virtually impossible to hit through this squad. So the rule should really read, "Choose the side of the court that you are comfortable playing." Any leftie-rightie combination is going to be rough for opponents, who must constantly remember where to lob and where to aim their serves, and they will face every kind of serve throughout the match. A leftie-rightie duo should automatically have an easier time holding their service games. What an advantage that is. Holding serve in doubles is even more important than holding serve in singles.

Travel

I've been on the road since 1975, going from city to city, country to country, and time zone to time zone. After a while you develop this endless traveling into high art. Now, you may never travel outside of your state to play tennis, but in case you ever do, I will give you my *Guide for the Girl on the Go*.

First, there is the packing. This is the part that de-presses me most about my life-style, because sometimes I am away for many weeks at a stretch, and I must live out of the suitcases I take with me. When the tour has been in one part of the world for any interesting length of time, it is possible to memorize everyone's wardrobe because you get so used to the outfits each person has packed for that circuit. We all get tired of our clothing and kid each other. We like to shop in the cities where we play to break up the tedium and add to our col-lections. In Italy a lot of leather is bought. In England it's sweaters; in Japan, watches. Players also take back from Japan stereos, televisions, tape players, and other electronic bargains, and the waiting line at airport customs is then a "Pack your lunch" proposition. I try to keep this sort of shopping down, and normally I can get by with packing one large suitcase, one tennis bag, and one hang-up bag for good clothes. Then, of course, there are my dogs—Tets, Ruby, and K.D. (Killer Dog). I love it when they are with me at tournaments, though I must admit that taking them along is a real production number.

Once I get to the airport, pick up the tickets, and arrange cages for the dogs, the hard part is over. I am a good flier, almost always being able to sleep on a flight. If I am going from the States to Japan or Australia or some other place with a radical time difference, I try to think myself into the other time while flying. On these long trips I drink a lot of fluids to prevent dehydration.

I like to stay at the official players' hotel, as long as the dogs are accepted. Transportation arrangements are simpler, and it's a lot easier to get in touch with people for practice when everyone's under the same roof. I will sometimes stay at a friend's house, which is a great and welcome change from the hotel scene. I don't mind hotels, but there is something nice about waking up in a familiar bed in familiar surroundings, using a big old bar of soap instead of all those annoying little ones, and being able to smell food cooking instead of getting the entire meal presented at once without the buildup of aroma. I love to cook and I miss the preparation process that seems to make the food taste even better.

As I check into the hotel I ask if there is room service twenty-four hours a day, and my follow-up question is always, "Is it any good?" Because I am in the singles and doubles of nearly every tournament and because scheduling puts me in the feature match most nights,

I rarely get back to the hotel before midnight. By then there's not much open and I feel like winding down anyway, so more than half my meals are eaten in my room. My three dogs have probably had more room service than most people, and they seem to enjoy hamburgers medium rare more than anything else on the menu. When I leave the room I make sure that they cannot get to the phone and call up for expensive bottles of wine. I absolutely refuse to let them get more spoiled than they already are.

Sometimes sleep does not come easy to me when I travel. It could be the hotel, or that I am nervous about a match, or that I'm nervous that I'm not asleep yet. If I just can't fall asleep I'll turn the light back on and read a book, and that usually does me in. You may have to experiment, because everyone is so different. If I am still sleepy before my match I'll take a little nap. There have been a few times that I was actually sleeping right up until an hour before I had to go on, but I thought that the nap would be worth it, and it was. You really have to know your own body, though. For some people a nap would just shut everything down too drastically, but for me the extra z's make all the difference. Just try not to press it, and relax as best you can, with or without the sleep.

I read the papers every day in whichever city I'm in, and being such a sports fan, I check out the sports pages pretty carefully. I always have been sensitive to what is written about me on and off the sports pages. Not that I always believe what they write about me— in some cities they don't even know me at all—but it makes me angry that writers have the power to say things about me so easily. I resent the awesome power of the press because so often it is misused, but there are some fine writers who truly know their subject—people like Rex Bellamy of the *Times* of London, Jane Levy in Washington, George Vescey and Ira Berkow of the *New York Times,* and Susan Baker Adams of *World Tennis* magazine. But so often ethics do not run high, and all I can do is shrug it off and turn the page to something else.

If you are playing tennis somewhere and you are asked for an interview for the local paper or television, do it. It will be a good experience for you to talk about yourself—your game, your life, and your goals—and you will learn how important media coverage can be to your career as well as to the success of the tournament. Try to be an open and easy interviewee and be conscious of the image you are projecting. That done, all you can do is hope for the best.

The biggest misconception people have about professional tennis is that all player expenses are paid for by someone else. We make our own flight arrangements and pay for tickets, make our own hotel bookings and pay the bill. We rent cars or take taxis, find the eating spots, wash our own laundry. Tennis is not at all like other professional sports, such as football or basketball, where the players don't worry about any of the details. They are handed their tickets at the gate, loaded onto the team bus, and simply deposit their dirty uniforms to be washed after each game. It's no small wonder that the younger players travel with friends, coaches, and parents. Life on the road can get pretty complicated. But more often than not, the terrific freedom you feel about your own destiny is worth all the trouble.

Housing at Tournaments

If you are fortunate enough to receive housing at a tennis tournament, be as good a house guest as you can be. Keep the room you are staying in very neat, and don't tie up or leave a mess in the bathroom. Do not make any long-distance phone calls at your host's expense. Offer to help with the chores, such as doing the dishes and cleaning your own laundry. Make certain that your housing people get passes to the matches, and if they are fans of the game and express interest, be thoughtful and courteous in answering any questions they may have. And last, be sure to write a thank-you letter after your stay. By keeping in touch you can develop a very nice friendship—there are many players on tour who return to certain cities year after year only because they have found enduring friendship there in a very transient life.

The Future of Tennis

For a while back in the 1970s the name of this game was "baseline." The top tennis player on the men's side was Bjorn Borg, whose relentless topspin ground-stroking gave him a stranglehold over all of his challengers. Chris Evert Lloyd enjoyed the same sort of mastery over the women, and she inspired countless young players to emulate her strokes, patience, and strategies. Bjorn and Chris were the role models, and it seemed as though every time a young boy played he'd pound open-stance loop forehands, while every young girl lined up her two-handed backhand and hit, again and again and then some more. Like any trend or fashion, people emulate those at the top.

Take a look around the game of tennis these days. The men's side is dominated by the power players— John McEnroe, Ivan Lendl, Jimmy Connors. John is my favorite. With all of his artistry, flair, and acrobatic ability, he takes the net away from his opponents and never gives it back. That is the way I like to play, and I believe that this brand of tennis is the tennis of the future. We are the champions that people model their games after. We play the aggressive, all-around game, and the only way to produce such tennis is to be in fine physical condition. The all-around game is electrifying to watch but extremely demanding to play. It took me a long time to realize that the style of tennis I love demanded more work than I ever dreamed of. It wasn't easy and it wasn't always fun, but I dedicated myself to the thought of becoming number one, of getting into the best physical condition of anyone to do so, and of working as hard as I could toward that goal. I have done all that. The work has paid off for me, and I feel even better about what is to come than what has gone by. I will only get stronger. Shouldn't you?

Glossary

Ace An untouched service winner.

Ad in The server's advantage.

Ad out The receiver's advantage.

Advantage The point following deuce. If the winner of the deuce point wins the advantage point, she wins the game; if she loses it, the score is once again deuce.

All-court game Playing all strokes from any part of the court.

Alley The area on each side of the singles court that is used for doubles.

American twist A serve in which the racket strikes upward on the ball, causing it to bounce high when it hits the ground.

Approach shot A forcing shot that enables a player to attack the net.

Australian formation ("I" formation) In doubles, the positioning of players so that the server's partner stands on the same side of the court as the server.

Babying the ball Patting the ball; hitting softly.

Backcourt The area from the service line to the baseline.

Backhand A groundstroke in which the ball is hit with the playing arm across the body.

Backswing The initial swing of the racket that prepares for the forward stroking motion.

Ball   That little round thing you hit in this game.

Ball boy   A person who retrieves balls for the players.

Baseline   The back line at either end of the tennis court.

Baseline game   The style of play whereby the player stays on or close to the baseline throughout and seldom advances to the net.

Big game   The style of play whereby the emphasis is on serving and volleying.

Broken service   A game won by the receiver.

Bye   The right given to seeded players at times to enter the next round without playing.

Caning the ball   Hitting the ball extremely hard.

Cannonball   A very fast and flat serve.

Center mark   The mark that bisects the baseline.

Center service line   The line that divides the two service courts in half.

Change of pace   The tactic of varying the speed of your shots or the spin of your shots.

Changing courts   The process whereby the players switch sides at the odd games during a set.

Choking   Folding under pressure.

Chop   A slicing stroke that gives a sharp backspin to the ball.

Circuit   The tour; the various events that make up a player's schedule.

Continental grip   A popular forehand grip that also can be used for the backhand.

Court   The playing area for tennis.

Cross-court   A stroke that drives the ball diagonally across the court.

Cruise control   A comfortable, nonvarying speed of play.

Dead ball   A ball that has been played out and destroyed by wear.

Deef   An abbreviation of the word "default."

Default   Victory given to a player whose opponent has declined to play or is absent for the start of the match.

Delivery   Service.

Deuce   An even score after 6 points.

Dink   A ball hit softly, usually from the short court.

Double fault   Two missed serves in a row.

Double hit   An illegal play where the ball is struck twice on the same play.

Doubles   A game with four players, two to a side.

Down-the-line   A ball hit parallel and close to the sideline.

Draw   The list of players in a tournament; also the act of deciding (by chance) the order in which the players will play, and against whom they will play.

Drive   A hard-hit groundstroke.

Drop   The unnatural downward curve that a topspin shot would make.

Drop volley   A volley hit softly, just over the net.

Dusting a player   Beating the player very easily.

Eastern grip   A common grip for a racket, used mostly for backhands.

Exhos   An abbreviation for exhibitions.

Fault   A served ball that does not strike in the service box.

Fifteen   A point scored by either player.

Five   The same as fifteen.

Flat serve   A very hard-hit serve with no spin.

Follow-through   The completion of the swing after the ball has been struck.

Foot fault   The improper positioning or movement of feet before or during the service motion.

Forecourt   The area between the service line and the net.

Forehand   The stroke used to hit a ball by a player on her right side if a rightie, her left side if a leftie.

Forty   Three points scored by either player.

Frame   The portion of the racket that holds the strings.

Fuzz   A tennis ball.

Game   The unit of scoring when a player has won 4 points, or has won by 2 after a deuce score.

Game point   The point that could give the game to the player leading in it.

Greasing out a match   Coming through a match mostly on luck.

Grip   The covering of the racket handle; also the manner of holding the racket in the hand.

Groundstroke   The stroke used to hit a ball after it has bounced.

Gut   An animal product, sometimes produced synthetically, used to string tennis rackets.

Gutsing out a match   Winning a match by using guts and courage.

Half volley   A stroke hit just as the ball is leaving the ground.

Handle   The end of the racket and the part you hold.

Head   The upper part of the racket to which the strings are attached.

Headhunter   A player who tries to blast the ball right at her opponent.

Hitting deep   Hitting close to the baselines.

Hitting over the ball   Imparting topspin.

Hitting short   Hitting the ball around the service area.

Holding serve   Winning a game while serving.

Hooking   Cheating.

Jamming   Playing in a practice session.

Let Any stroke that does not count and is played over. In serving, a ball that touches the net and goes into the proper court, also requiring a replay.

Lines The markings that indicate the boundaries of the court.

Linesmen The officials in a match who decide if balls are in or out.

Lob A stroke played high in the air.

Lob volley A volley hit over the head of the opponent.

Long Shots outside the service lines or baselines.

Loop A ball that travels in an arc rather than a straight line.

Love A scoring term meaning zero.

Love game A game in which one side failed to score a point.

Love set A set in which a player did not win a single game.

Match A predetermined number of sets that will decide a winner. For women it is usually two out of three; for men it is usually three out of five.

Match point The final point in a match.

Midcourt The area around the service line.

Mixed doubles A match between two teams, each consisting of one male and one female.

Net The netting across the middle of the court.

Netman The doubles player who stands close to the net as an opponent serves.

No-man's-land The area between the baseline and the service line where a player should not stand to wait for the ball.

Not up A double bounce. The call made by the official is "not up."

Out   A ball that lands outside of the playing area.

Overhead   A shot hit with the racket above the head, normally off a lob.

Pace   The speed of play or the speed of the ball.

Passing shot   A stroke that drives the ball past an opponent at net.

Pet shots   A player's favorite shots.

Poach   At net, hitting a ball in doubles that should have been played by one's partner.

Point of impact   The point at which the racket meets the ball.

Powdering a ball   Hitting a ball as hard as possible.

Press   To force and attack an opponent.

Puff player   A player who hits a soft ball.

Pusher   Like a puff player, one who merely returns balls relentlessly.

Putaway   A shot hit so well that no return is made.

Qualies   An abbreviation for qualifying rounds.

Racket   The implement used to hit the ball.

Rallying   A series of groundstrokes.

Ready position   The proper way to stand while waiting for the ball—weight forward, knees bent, racket in position.

Receiver   The player who receives service.

Referee   The chief official in a tennis match.

Retire   Default; refusing to continue a match.

Runner-up   The final-round loser in an event.

Rushing the net   A strategy in which the player advances to the net after hitting the ball.

Seeding   Placements of the best players in a tournament so that they do not meet one another early in the tournament.

Semifinal One of the two matches in the round before the final.

Serve The act of putting the ball into play.

Server The player who puts the ball into play.

Set The unit of scoring whereby a player has won six games at least by two games or has won a tie breaker.

Set point The game point that will also win the set.

Setup An easy shot that a player can hit for an outright winner.

Sidelines The lines at either side of the court that mark the outside boundaries of the playing field.

Sidespin A spin that causes the ball to bounce to one side.

Singles A game played one against one.

Sleaze ball A terribly lucky shot that has somehow gone over the net.

Slice A stroke hit with sidespin.

Smash Overhead.

Spin The rotation of a ball in flight.

Spoon up on a ball Carrying the ball with the racket face, usually on the stretch.

Stop volley A volley intended to drop barely over the net.

Sudden death A method of scoring used at six-games-all to decide the winner of the set.

"T" The middle line bisecting the service court.

Taking the hill Playing the net.

Tanking a match (also "tossing a match") Giving up, not even trying.

Thirty In scoring, a term used to denote 2 points.

Threading the needle Hitting a passing shot between the opponent and the sideline.

Topspin To hit the ball on its top surface, producing a forward, revolving motion.

Toss Throwing the ball in the air to begin a serve. Also, the method used to determine which player will serve first and which receive first in a match. This is normally done by spinning the racket.

Treeing ("in the trees") A player who is playing so well that she is off the ground and in the trees as she plays. *See* Zoning.

Umpire The official in charge of a tournament.

Volley A stroke made by intercepting the ball before it has touched the ground.

Western grip A method of gripping the racket.

Wood shot A shot that does not strike the strung portion of the racket.

Work on the ball The heavy slice that has been imparted on a shot.

Zoning Like treeing, zoning is when a player plays beyond her normal games for a time and produces uncharacteristically fine tennis. That player is "in the zone."

Index

Note: Page numbers in italics refer to illustrations.